Westward Adventure

11, 089

Westward Adventure

THE TRUE STORIES OF SIX PIONEERS

William O. Steele

Maps by Kathleen Voute

Harcourt, Brace & World, Inc., New York

Library of Congress Catalog Card Number: 62-9479

Printed in the United States of America

First edition

Contents

6 *Contents*

A Word Before

Having attained a foothold along the Atlantic Coast, the English colonists in North America might have been content to stay there, at least for some time. They might have continued as a crown colony for centuries and kept their faces turned dutifully toward the sea and toward their native land. But there were those who couldn't resist stealing a quick glance over their shoulders. What did they see?

Some, like the New England clergyman and poet Michael Wigglesworth, saw:

> "A waste and howling wilderness,
>   Where none inhabited
> But hellish fiends, and brutish men
>   That devils worshiped."

Many looked and liked what they saw. And these began to leave the settlements along the Atlantic fringe and push farther westward.

Geography—the mountains and rivers—and the presence of hostile Indian tribes dictated the way this expansion should go. But why did it begin to move?

Someone once tried to prove that all forms of life instinctively go in a direction "contrary to that of a moving rotating object upon which they are placed." If this were true, plants, animals, and man would have to go westward on this revolving earth.

Surely though, on the American continent, man pushed inland and westward for better reasons than instinct. Why then?

The Indian thought he knew the answer—land! And though he never understood the individual ownership of land, he could see that year by year the English colonists were forcing him to give up his hunting lands and the river valleys where he and his ancestors had long lived. The Indian was realizing that no matter how much land white men got, they were never satisfied; they always wanted more and more.

When the commander of Fort Loudoun on the Little Tennessee River was captured by the Cherokees, he was tortured and dirt was stuffed into his mouth, fistfuls of it. One of the Cherokee chiefs screamed, "You want land, we will give it to you."

Yet, land was not the only reason men moved into that area called the Old Southwest—that unbounded region south and west of the Thirteen Colonies. No, there were all sorts of reasons. The reasons men do things, even the same things, are always many and varied.

This book is not a history of colonization or of the moving frontier. It is a book of true stories of different types of people and of their troubles and purposes in pushing through and around the Appalachian Mountains into the land of the Western Waters. This is a thrust of adventure.

Westward Adventure

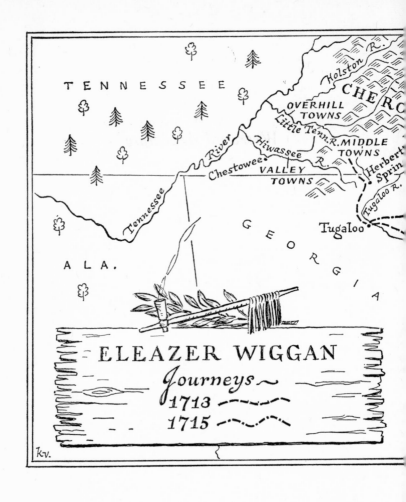

~ *Part One* ~

Eleazer Wiggan, Indian trader, known as the Old Rabbit, with some accounts of his life between 1713 and 1715.

1

Where the Atlantic Ocean Begins

The Old Rabbit, as Eleazer Wiggan was called by the Cherokees, was leaving Charles Town, in the colony of South Carolina, to trade in the vast Indian country. He led a string of six pack horses loaded with "tinsey" lace, "half thicks," calico petticoats, Duffield blankets, and other truck. He was headed north across South Carolina and then over the Appalachian Mountains to the towns of the Cherokee Indians four hundred miles away.

He turned and looked a little wistfully at the two-story brick dwellings, at the cypress plank houses with their tile roofs, and down the street to where the ships were anchored by the warehouses. One last look.

Ahead of him was a long, hard journey—*if* he reached the Indian nation safely. And he might not make it to his destination. That was a hazard of traveling. In 1713 any person using the paths that led into the interior of North America could count on not only plenty of troubles but also many dangers along the route.

The Old Rabbit jerked on the lead horse's rope and turned into King Street. He moved off toward the northern outskirts of Charles Town in the bright May sunshine. The bells, tied to the animals' bridles, jingled as the horses plodded along through the dust behind him.

The streets were filled with people, for the Indian trade made Charles Town a lively place every spring. Traders were here to sell peltry the Indians had taken in the fall and winter hunts. Merchants bought these skins and furs and packed the heaviest and best ones into casks to ship to England, to be used in making clothing and in covering trunks and boxes. "South Carolina hats," worn in England about this time, were called that because they were made from the deerskins shipped from Charles Town.

The lighter deerskins and the poorer ones were used locally for the making of saddles, shoes, and breeches. What was unwanted for the town's leather industries was shipped to New England or some other northern colony.

So the spring months were busy times. The taverns and punch houses had roistering Indian traders drinking to Queen Anne's health in pewter tankards and watching the entertainment—feats of legerdemain and traveling shows of "Ourangnogang (or Man of the Woods)." There were games of bowls, skittles and nine pins, or cockfighting for visitors. Those who preferred more active sports could fight the sailors thronging the streets from the British men-of-war anchored in the harbor or beat up the men of the constable's watch.

The Old Rabbit shifted his gun to his right hand and took the pack horse's lead rope in his other. It was hot, and sweat was already beginning to run down his neck and under his woolen shirt. A gull wheeled overhead, screaming. A colored woman with a basket of shrimp on her head darted in front of him. A man pushing a wheelbarrow loaded with cedar shingles wobbled to one side out of the way of the pack train.

Coming down King Street toward Wiggan were six tall Indians. They stepped haughtily along, looking neither to left nor to right, their faces stiff and solemn. Beads and shells and feathers were twisted into their scalp locks. The leader wore a feather cloak and carried some kind of wand in his hands, held out before him. The others, in single file behind him, wore white fur capes and soft-looking doeskin mocassins. Below each knee all had garters of shells.

The Old Rabbit looked at them closely, but he could not tell by their dress to what tribe they belonged. They might be a peace delegation from the Chickasaws living along the Mississippi River way to the west. Or it might be these were Hitchiti representatives seeking aid against the Spanish in Florida. Or perhaps Natchez from the lands around the Gulf.

A white man trailed them, but the Old Rabbit did not know him. He knew, though, that these Indians and their white interpreter were heading for the place where the Board of Commissioners met "for regulating the Indian Trade and making it safe to the Publick."

These nine white men of Charles Town had plenty of business to transact this time of the year. Traders came to their meetings to complain about Indians stealing their wares, agents to tell of distant tribes that wanted the colony's trade, Indians to protest about the traders' horses eating their corn or the high price of the trade goods offered them, and many other matters.

Wiggan had just been before them to get a "fresh license." It was paid and his bond money put up for another year of trading among the Indians.

Charles Town was the center of an Indian trade that spread out across the entire southern part of the continent. Beyond the Appalachians, in the valleys of the Tennessee and the lower Mississippi Rivers and on the broad plains of the Gulf, the Carolina trader reached with his trading goods. This was the chief business of the colony, and deerskins were the main export. It was so important to South Carolina that the Indian trade was heavily regulated, and the nine commissioners did their best to keep it properly organized and at the same time extend it by taking trade away from the French.

In 1713, the town was the fourth largest in the twelve colonies and the only southern British seaport. Over three thousand people were crowded onto the lower tip of the peninsula, where the Ashley and Cooper Rivers came together to form the harbor. The merchants were getting rich from the Indian trade, and the town was expanding fast. There was a boast that Charles Town was the place where the Ashley and Cooper met to form the Atlantic Ocean.

The Old Rabbit knew that it was much too expensive a place for a smalltime trader like himself to stay. "Lodging and dyet" cost a man too much in such dear and scarce times. He was leaving the town broke, but he was leaving thoughtful too. It would take a man of "parts and temper" to make a fortune in the Indian trade. He wanted to do this, but how?

That was the question he pondered as he left Charles Town for another year of trading, left the important officials and wealthy merchants to pace their garden walks in periwigs and knee breeches and satin waistcoats. There must be some way a simple Indian trader could make some quick money.

But how?

2

Bewitching Western Waters

The Old Rabbit traveled fast that first day, splashing headlong across the many creeks and through the swamps of the Carolina low country till he was wet to the waist. He stopped only once, and that was when he met an Indian medicine man from Keowee, a town of the Lower Cherokees.

The priest was dressed in a white man's pants and shirt. He wore his hair in two long braids. Though old and wrinkled, he stood straight. He greeted Wiggan with dignity.

The trader tied his horses so that the animals could graze and then took out a wallet of tobacco. From a skin bag at his belt the Indian produced a pipe. The two squatted there in the narrow trail and silently smoked, handing the Indian's pipe back and forth.

At last the medicine man stood and said he was going

to Charles Town to complain to the commissioners. A trader had tried to make him carry a bundle of skins, and when the old Indian refused, the white man had beat him with a stick.

The Indian carefully took off the dirty white shirt, with its lacy ruffles up the front, and showed Wiggan his cut and bruised back. The Old Rabbit sympathized with him.

The medicine man said that the trader had also taken his conjuring crystal with which he could foretell the future. Wiggan had never seen one of these stones, but he had heard that one of the priests of the Middle Towns of the Cherokees had a magical stone he kept in an earthen jar. It was hidden in a secret cave back in the mountains, and once every week the priest fed it blood.

No medicine man would part with his magical crystal no matter how much stroud cloth and vermilion paint was offered. The Old Rabbit was not much interested in anything he couldn't bargain over. Let the Charles Town Indian commissioners worry over this. He gave the old Indian a handful of tobacco, bade him farewell, and moved on with his horses.

By the middle of the fifth day, he reached Savannah Town. Here were stockades and traders' houses and, surrounding them, along both banks of the Savannah River, the huts of the Indians. This was the chief inland base of the Carolina Indian trade. A trader could buy horses here or a dugout canoe to take his skins to Charles Town. He could hire Indian burdeners or a white man to help him with his pack horses. And he could take one of the many Indian paths that spread out from this spot in all directions across the southern part of the continent.

As there was still half a day's traveling time left, Wiggan did not stop. He turned onto the trail that led upstream along the east bank and left behind this trading post built at the falls of the Savannah River.

It had rained recently, and the way was slippery and muddy as he wound in and out among the many cane brakes. He kept a sharp lookout for rattlesnakes. The Cherokees would go around one in the path and leave it unharmed, but Wiggan believed in killing every one he saw. He had once seen a man die of a rattler's bite.

The wolves were bad later that night. They hung around the camp, just outside the firelight, and snapped their jaws and sniffled. Wiggan had to bring his hobbled horses in close and it up and guard them.

But it wasn't th ake and other vermin" he worried about when "gadding abroad" along the trails of the back country. No, it was a white man fleeing from the high sheriff, who might wait behind a fallen tree and shoot him in the back as he passed. Or it could be one Indian, or more, waiting at the fording place of a stream for him. Six pack horses loaded with truck were a tempting fortune.

The next morning Wiggan crossed a stream and sloshed up the opposite bank, remembering how two Yamasee Indians had jumped him once right here. They had been all who were left of a war party, and they didn't want to return home without some booty. Wiggan had used his fusil, the light flint musket he carried. He had shot one of the Indians in the leg and clubbed the second with his heavy flintlock pistol.

The next day's traveling was much easier. The trail led through scattered pine forests. Once he took some of the sticky gum and smeared it on a cut on one of the pack horse's flanks. He shot at a turkey in the late afternoon, but he missed and went hungry to bed that night, his corn and pease having given out long since.

He crossed the Savannah River at Tugaloo, "the most Antient Town in these parts." It was a Lower Cherokee town, where many paths came together and several traders lived.

Wiggan gossiped with one of the traders for a short while. Then putting a fresh charge of powder in his fusil and pistol, he set off once more. The Appalachian Mountains stretched in a rugged blue line ahead of him. Soon the path was rough and he had to slow his pace.

Less than a week later he was among tall beeches, their trunks bright and silvery. Purple rhododendron and flaming azalea and late silver bells bloomed along the path.

Wiggan followed the winding trail to a low gap in the mountains. This place was a divide. Behind him were the waters that flowed into the Atlantic Ocean. Ahead were the rivers and creeks that were called the "Western Waters." These flowed westward and eventually ended in the Mississippi River.

There was a spring just ahead of Wiggan and below the gap's summit. This was later to be called Herbert's Spring after an Indian commissioner. Here was "ye hade of a nother River that Rones into masashipey." The Old Rabbit hurried toward it, for he had decided to eat his noonday meal beside the cold, fast-flowing spring and to rest his pack horses.

At the spring, he found another trader and his helper with eight Indian slaves. Each Indian had a rope tied around the neck and around both arms above the elbows, and each one was tied securely to a larger rope, which ran from the first slave to the last. They were sitting to one side of the spring as Wiggan approached.

The Old Rabbit greeted the trader and learned who he was and that these were Sara Indians, whom the Cherokees had taken on a war raid and had then sold to the trader. He was now taking them to the slave market in Charles Town. Indians made poor workers in the plantation fields, and those sold as slaves were usually shipped out to the other colonies or to the West Indies.

The slave trader drank from the spring and stood up and wiped his mouth. Wiggan laughed and told him that he was doomed—that whoever drank from this spring would have to return to the Cherokee nation and the saying went that he would not be able to leave there for seven years. For, said Wiggan, these Western Waters had such a natural bewitching quality that they affected one in that fashion.

The slave trader grunted contemptuously. He said the water didn't taste like much to him. And he would call it French water anyway, for every one knew it flowed toward the lands claimed by the French. The Mississippi and all the other inland waters belonged to the French, or soon would. The French were already in Settico, he'd heard, and had persuaded that Overhill Cherokee town to renounce the English.

The Overhill Cherokee were settled along the lower part of the Little Tennessee River. The French and their Indian allies came there often to try to induce the Cherokees to trade with Frenchmen.

Wiggan was not much worried. He figured the English trade goods were better quality than those offered by the French, and the Cherokees knew it. Besides, there were always wild rumors about the French. He would not believe them. He knew the head man of Settico was true to the English.

Wiggan drank from the spring and offered the other man and his helper some venison. They ate and discussed the prices of skins and slaves. The Old Rabbit asked him how much these slaves might bring in Charles Town.

The slave trader answered that he would likely get between four and five hundred pounds sterling, for they were all young men and women and therefore could stand hard work. Slaves over thirty years of age did not bring nearly so much at the market.

Wiggan sat silently musing for a while. At last the slave trader stood up and yelled at the Indians to get to their feet. They began to rise. But the last one in line, a young warrior, was slow. His slowness angered the slave trader. He went over and kicked the Indian. The red man did not flinch, nor did he move any faster. Languidly he rose to his feet and stood at ease staring out into the distance. The trader's helper started them moving along the trail.

Wiggan watched the group till they were out of sight. Indian slaves were certainly a quick way to fortune, but it would be better for a man to capture his own than to buy them for reselling. Should he try it?

He moved off down the slope with his trade goods, toward the Middle Cherokee settlements along the upper portion of the Little Tennessee River. The bewitching Western Waters had brought him back one more time to these inland Indians.

But brought him back to what—to fortune or to poverty?

3

"*A Sortment of Goods for the Indian Trade*"

In a little over a fortnight Wiggan had reached the Cherokees of the Middle Towns, the heart of the nation on the headwaters of the Tuckasegee and the Little Tennessee Rivers. If he continued on to the Overhill Towns, across another range in the Appalachians, there would be another week of traveling.

It is not known where the Old Rabbit lived among the Cherokees in 1713. He must have had a house in one town and traded there, as well as in many of the other scattered villages and in those of the Yuchi Indians, as did other traders. In later years, when the trade was much more regulated, each trader was given one or two towns in which to trade, and no one else was supposed to compete with him there.

In such later times a trader became an important man in the Indian community. He often married one of the chief's daughters and was taken into the tribe with the proper ceremonies. Then he voted on matters affecting the tribe, whether to go to war, what messages to send to the various colonial governors, and so on.

By withholding guns and ammunition he could exert a tremendous pressure on the tribes. He might have Negro slaves, and most certainly he would raise pigs and cows and keep many horses. He was treated like a king, and if he used his influence wisely, he was much loved by the Indians. Still, he could never expect to become wealthy, not in the white man's sense.

Wherever Wiggan lived, when he arrived, he would begin to unload his six pack horses at his store. It might be he lived in one house and did his trading in another building right beside it. However, the houses would be just like the other rectangular dwellings in the town.

The Cherokees built their houses as they had always done. Posts were set upright in the ground a few feet apart. Long canes, or slender saplings if these were easier to obtain, were woven in and out between the posts, and sometimes cane mats were used too. Then mud, but better, clay, was plastered over the canes and the posts, both inside and out. If the family was extra tidy, it might whitewash the walls with decayed mussel shells. The roof was made of thatched grass or slabs of tree bark, with a hole in the center for the smoke to escape.

That would be what was known as the summer house. In really cold weather a small round hothouse, built of the same materials as the summer one but partly underground, was used. Inside a fire was kept burning all the time, and the members of the family slept on tiers around the sides.

At more important trading spots, like Savannah Town, the houses of the colony's officials would be built in the typical English fashion of frame construction. This required much sawing of boards and squaring of joists. It took the services of a carpenter, too, and usually of two sawyers, and the hauling of them and their saws, hammers, various axes, and nails was very costly, as were their salaries.

The Old Rabbit would most certainly not have had a cabin made of whole logs, notched and fitted together at the corners. This Swedish invention was not yet widespread and was foreign at this time to the English colonists of the south. It would take the frontier families leapfrogging into the wilderness later in the eighteenth century to use and spread this type of dwelling.

In all probability the Old Rabbit's "store" was simply a Cherokee cane, post, and clay house, with his goods ranged around the walls or across empty barrels and on cane mats and tarpaulin on the floor. If competition with other traders was keen, trouble was taken to display the items, and always the goods must be kept dry and locked up.

Most pack horses could carry about two hundred pounds. Since the trade goods were of various sizes, shapes, and weights, Wiggan had placed on each horse a variety of items, trying not to overload the animal or to make the load so bulky as to be difficult to transport. Now he took all the bundles from the packsaddles and carried them inside his store. He fed and watered his horses, then set about sorting out the merchandise for display.

He began with the muskets. He might have brought these in two pieces and later fitted the wooden stock to the barrel with metal pins and a tang screw. Otherwise, the guns would have had to be specially packed to keep them from snagging on the vines and limbs crowding the sides of the narrow trails.

Anyway, the guns would receive special attention from any trader. These were his high-priced item and always in demand. The price varied with the years, but around this time an Indian could get a musket for thirty-five deerskins.

A gun was the first of the white man's possessions the red man wanted. In fact, he had to have it to keep from being old-fashioned. He was happy to forget his former weapons, the stone-age bow and arrow. And as he used the gun more and more, he forgot not only how to shoot the bow and arrow with skill but how to make them properly too. It ceased to matter that formerly he had been able to fire six or seven arrows in a minute, while with the musket he might manage with luck to fire twice in the same length of time, and then nowhere near so accurately.

When Wiggan got his trading guns arranged in his storehouse, he unpacked the pistols, each of which was worth about twenty skins. If he had not bothered to make shelves, he placed these on a low platform similar to those on which the Cherokees slept. There was not too great a demand for pistols, nor for swords, for which he received ten skins. But he would have a few of each on hand anyway.

He took the coats next. The Old Rabbit unfolded them and shook them out carefully. A "broadcloth coat, laced" or "a double striped Cloth Coat, Tinsey laced" was worth almost as much as a gun. Whenever the Indian commissioners in Charles Town gave a present to an Indian for some service rendered, it was most often a fancy coat.

Sometimes a hat was added to the gift, seldom breeches though. Generally, Indian men felt that the white man's breeches made them helpless and effeminate. The Indian women called the wearing of breeches "that pinching custom." Usually the closer to the white settlements a tribe lived, the quicker they took to wearing breeches, though they liked loose-fitting ones.

The coats were made of many different fabrics: "half thicks" (a kind of worsted cloth), stroud (a cheap woolen cloth made in Stroud, Gloucestershire, England, and sometimes called Stroudwater), and "plains" (flannel). The Indians didn't seem to care what kinds of material were used, just so long as it was a coat, preferably brightly colored and decorated.

Men didn't get all the white man's goods. Cherokee women had plenty of say-so in the tribe's affairs and in the homes. Wiggan would have brought quantities of glass beads, calico petticoats, white and red and blue and striped Duffield blankets, bags of sugar, gilt leather girdles or red ones, scissors, salt, mirrors, and caddis ribbon of worsted yarn.

There was tinsey lace too, which was made of silk or wool and had gold or silver threads running through it. There were plenty of goodies for all with skins to trade; the traders as well as the town merchants saw to that.

Of course there were ordinary but useful items like hoe blades (broad and narrow), brass kettles, butcher knives, axes, and so on. One of the most interesting things mentioned in later times was "double-jointed babies"— probably dolls.

The Indian seemed happy to trade his skins for almost anything of the white man's as long as he felt he wasn't being cheated and the wares were of good quality. He didn't always use the goods in the way they were meant to be used, though. A brave might buy a pair of scissors with one deerskin and, having little to cut with them, end up wearing them as an ornament on a thong around his neck. Who cared? It was his skin; let him spend it as he wanted and shape the white man's belongings to his own personal use.

Deerskins, "clean trimmed, free from Snouts and

Shanks," were usually what the Indian offered in payment. The traders took other skins too, but deerskins were the most common because there were so many deer and they were easy to stalk and kill.

An early traveler had been amazed at the great number of deer in Carolina, "such infinite Herds that the whole Country seems but one continued Park." It is amazing still to know that between 1699 and 1715 Charles Town exported an average of fifty-four thousand deerskins yearly. This was before the trade had expanded to take in a great number of Indian tribes. Later, when trading was more highly organized, the merchants sent to England in one year one hundred and sixty thousand deerskins. These were of course the best skins. How many more were used locally and shipped to northern colonies is not known.

Beaver skins were desired abroad, but the southern climate was much milder than that of the north, and consequently the pelt of the beaver was not so thick in the south and was not so sought after. Too, some Indians such as the Choctaw and the Chickasaw, refused to hunt the beaver, although it was plentiful in their land. They said it was only fit quarry for women and white men, not for warriors.

Buffalo skins were wanted but were not a trade item in the early part of the eighteenth century because the buffalo had not yet spread out widely over the southeastern part of the continent. Traders were always hoping for a buffalo robe, though, to give as a special present to an official. They sometimes bought them from Indians who had been hunting further west along the Cumberland or along the Ohio River.

Deerskins were traded in "raw" or untanned condition. These did not bring as much as dressed skins, those that had been scraped and worked with animal brains by the Indian women, then smoked till they were soft and supple and light in color. The deer was fattest and his coat heaviest in the fall and winter, and that was when the Indians went on long hunts together.

Now the Old Rabbit had returned to set up his store once again on the Western Waters. It was June, and there was little business to do. Most of the skins had already been bargained away. What little trading was done during the summer months more than likely was done on credit.

But Wiggan could go fishing with the red men, take to the warpath, watch their ball games, sit and gossip with the young warriors, or listen to the tales of the medicine men and storytellers.

Then one day into Wiggan's town came a trader named Alexander Long from Euphase, a town on the upper part of the Hiwassee River. He dropped by to visit with Wiggan and tell of his troubles.

Long was furious with the Yuchi Indians who lived in a few small villages on the lower part of the Hiwassee River. He had credited those at Chestowee with some goods, and now they would not pay him for them. He had had an argument with one of the Yuchi braves from Chestowee, and the red man had attacked Long and taken off a part of his scalp.

Long said he was going to get revenge, that he had sworn Chestowee "shoold be cut off before green Corne Time." Late August or early September was when the Green Corn Celebration took place. How was he going to destroy the town by then?

Wiggan was silent.

Long went on to say that he didn't know how he was going to get the Cherokees to help him lay waste to Chestowee, but that he was angry enough to either kill all the Yuchis there or make slaves of them. However, he needed help.

Slaves. Wiggan sat up, looking interested. Did Long think there would be many slaves if the town was attacked?

Long replied that he thought there would be "a brave Parcel of Slaves if Chestowe were cut off."

Wiggan pondered. This could be the chance for which he had been waiting.

4

"A Brave Parcel of Slaves"

It was late August and the Yuchi town of Chestowee was quiet in the early morning darkness. A breeze stirred over the Hiwassee River and moved off to rattle the leaves and sway the green ears of corn growing along the banks.

Wooden pirogues bumped together lightly as the water rippled along the town's landing place.

There was a movement among the trees outside the town. A prowling dog sniffed suspiciously, then moved toward the bushes with a low growl. A tomahawk crushed in its skull, and all was still again.

It grew lighter. What had been shadows a moment ago were now Cherokee braves in war paint waiting behind trees, squatting among the bushes, hiding among the corn stalks. They had surrounded the town except for a short stretch along the river.

The white traders, Long and Wiggan, were there, too. They had talked the Cherokees of Hiwassee and a few others of the Middle Towns into coming on this war party. They had supplied the Indians freely with powder and lead. Long hoped for revenge on the Yuchis before the morning was gone. He hoped for slaves, too, and Wiggan was with him in that wish.

Now smoke came from the roof holes in many of the dwellings. A woman came out of one of the houses and went toward the river. She scooped up water in a brass trade pot and turned back. A child had followed her. She called to it, and the child shook its head and ran toward the cornfield where a group of Cherokees crouched.

Wiggan nudged Long. They got to their feet. Long gave a war whoop. The Cherokees charged from their hiding places, shooting and yelling.

Yuchi men appeared before their houses, surprised and

sleepy-eyed. Some had guns and some had tomahawks, but many were empty-handed. The battle to cut off Chestowee had started.

Between the houses and across the town square hand-to-hand fighting raged. A few Yuchi dashed for the dugout boats and got away. A mother and her two children crept unnoticed into the cornfield and escaped unharmed.

The sound of firing was loud. Now the Yuchi houses were burning, and the crackling of the fire added to the din. Smoke rose above the village and hung there, red as blood from the sunrise.

A small group fought their way to the council house: an old man shooting arrows; boys and women swinging hoes and sticks and broken muskets; several warriors firing their guns furiously. They reached the large building and barricaded themselves inside.

Many of the Yuchis had already given themselves up. Wiggan and Long guarded them. Half of the houses were aflame. There were only scattered shots here and there. The last of the struggle took place around the council house.

There had been much shooting at first from those inside. But suddenly it was quiet. The Cherokees surrounding the council house waited. Not a sound came from within. Finally several braves rushed up and battered in the door. No shots sounded; no whoops or challenges echoed from the council building.

The Cherokees readied their tomahawks and guns and dashed into the building. Inside in the dimness lay men, women, and children who had killed themselves rather than fall into the hands of the Cherokees. The battle was over. The Yuchis were driven away, never again to live in Chestowee.

The Cherokees buried their own dead, took the Yuchi scalps and plunder, and headed home. Long and Wiggan went with them, guarding the captive Yuchis. They had their "brave Parcel of Slaves."

5

Cherokee Question Mark

The Old Rabbit did not get rich from selling his slaves. The Indian commissioners ordered him and Long to turn the Yuchi Indians loose. The traders' licenses and the money posted for their bonds were revoked. The Cherokees involved were not punished, as it was felt they had been tricked into this wrong-doing.

This one incident was the worst thing Eleazer Wiggan did in his lifetime of trading, and he soon redeemed himself.

In the spring of 1715, the southern Indians revolted against the many abuses of the traders and the harsh policies of the South Carolina government. "The Calamity of Warr was first fomented by some of the lower Creeke people, but the first stroke was given by the Yamasees." So this became the Yamasee War.

Traders were murdered, some tortured; their stores were broken into and the goods plundered. The border plantations were burned, the livestock slaughtered. The many Indian tribes leagued together to bring fire and destruction to the colony.

The white settlers fled to Charles Town at the first alarm. The situation soon became desperate. The peninsula was overcrowded, food gave out, and the army could not stop the Indian raids.

Salvation depended on two great inland tribes—the Creeks and the Cherokees. The Creeks had struck once and were expected to attack again any day. But the Cherokees were a question mark. What would they do?

The Cherokees must be persuaded to join the colonists against the Creeks. These two nations had always been enemies. But who would risk his life in traveling to the Cherokee towns? Who would go among them on such a dangerous mission?

Eleazer Wiggan would. He volunteeered and the colony accepted, offering him trade goods, horses, and a promise of five hundred pounds in money if he persuaded the Cherokees to help South Carolina in the war.

Another trader, Robert Gilcrest, went also. They set out in late summer through the deserted countryside. The Savannah River route was too dangerous to travel. The Creeks would surely ambush them somewhere along it. So the two took instead another trail that went along the Congaree and Saluda Rivers to the Lower Towns of the Cherokees.

Wiggan had tied extra bells on the horses. He wanted

the Cherokees to hear him coming. It would show them he wasn't afraid, that he came in peace and without deceit.

Tugaloo was the capital of the nation at this time, and the two traders went there. As they entered the town, braves gathered around them, threatening them with tomahawks and scalping knives and guns. Women screamed at them and beat at them with sticks. The children threw rocks. One of the horses was slashed with a knife. The crowd grew larger and larger.

Wiggan and Gilcrest kept an outward calm, though it looked bad for them. Suddenly the Cherokees gave way, and the Conjurer, chief of the town, came up with several of the old men. They listened to what the Old Rabbit had to say, and they agreed to a meeting of the head men. Messages were sent to the other towns to summon them to Tugaloo.

The two traders were given a house. As they made their way to it, they saw no friendly faces. The Old Rabbit was grim. He would have to use some mighty persuasion at the meeting, else he and Gilcrest would be killed and the Cherokees would take to the warpath against the colony.

As the fall days passed and the leaves turned, the white men were busy. Gilcrest bestowed ribbons, lace, and strips of stroud cloth on the wives of prominent chiefs. The Conjurer had a broken musket. Wiggan gave him a new gun, fixed the old one, and presented it to his son.

When the Cherokees arrived from the other towns, Wiggan pressed gifts of powder and lead upon them, gave them strings of glass beads to take home to their wives. He saw to it that each chief received a scarlet coat and fancy hat. And he talked and talked, recalling old times, hunts they had had together, or evenings telling stories around a fire with old friends and old friendliness.

Many refused his gifts and would not talk to him. But he listened courteously to all who would talk, and he kept his good humor.

At last the meeting took place. It was a chilly fall night. The stars were bright overhead and the crickets chirped loudly. The town was very quiet. It was a solemn and important occasion.

The meeting was at the council house. This was a building on the west side of the town square, used as a temple for religious ceremonies or as a place for business gatherings. It was a large peaked building with seven sides, one for each of the Cherokee clans.

Inside, it was dark. There was a small fire in the center of the floor, but it offered little light. This was the sacred fire that was never allowed to go out. Around the center were the seats, rising one above the other.

Wiggan and Gilcrest took their places across from the principal chiefs. The house was almost filled with Indians. Occasionally the fire would blaze up and Wiggan would find black eyes staring at him coldly.

After they had smoked, Wiggan was asked to explain his mission. He told how treacherous the Creeks were, how the Creeks killed Cherokees all the time and stole their women. He reminded the chiefs that South Carolina was their friend and wanted to help them. He ended by asking that they vote to go to war with the colonists against the Creeks.

One chief rose to say that the friendship of the Carolinians lasted no longer than the presents they gave. As soon as the presents wore out, the friendship was forgotten.

Another war chief said they should join the Creeks, whip the colonists, then turn and wipe out all Creeks. He wanted to torture the two traders that night.

An old headman told the young warriors not to forget that times had changed since the old days, that the Cherokees could no longer do without the white man and his guns and his metal tools.

And so the talk went on hour after hour through the night. Each Indian who wanted to speak was allowed an opportunity. Wiggan answered their charges, he pleaded with them, but he did not let them taunt him into anger.

Still, the Indians were unpredictable, and Wiggan knew it. He was very worried. It appeared as if the Conjurer and the Lower Towns would vote for helping the colony. The chief of Echota, whom the whites had named Caesar, was wavering. But there were many, he felt sure, who would vote against joining the white man, no matter how much they hated the Creeks.

At last it was time to vote. When the final tally was counted, Wiggan drew a long breath of relief. He had won. A group of headmen and some hundred warriors decided to accompany him to Charles Town.

The Cherokee question mark was erased.

6

The White Man's Path

The Yamasee War came to an end when the Cherokees offered their aid to the whites. A few raids continued from widespread Indian groups, but the colony was at peace and saved. The Carolinians went back to the border areas they had left at the first outbreak of hostilities. The government began friendly negotiations with the many Indian nations. South Carolina had won the war, but the cost left many gloomy. One Carolinian wrote, "We are just now the poorest Colony in all America and have both before us at Sea and behind us at Land very distracting appearances of ruine."

For that reason, the mainstay of South Carolina's commerce—trading—could not be given up. Much effort was devoted to recapturing their former lucrative position. The Old Rabbit was willing to aid in this, and he went back to trading. He never mistreated the Cherokees, though he liked to annoy the Indian commissioners and outsmart them.

Once, at the Indian Board's request, he came to Charles Town and stayed a month. He lived at the best inns and wined and dined in a truly kingly manner—and sent all the bills to the Indian Board. There was nothing the board could do except pay the bills. But they hastily passed a law making it impossible for any trader ever again to entertain himself at the board's expense.

The records contain many such Wiggan incidents. The white officials often found him annoying, while the Indians shrugged off these happenings as purely mischievous. The Cherokees understood him and gave him the nickname of Cheesto Kaiehre, the Old Rabbit.

The rabbit appears in many of the Cherokee folk tales as a mischief maker, a trickster just like Brer Rabbit in the Uncle Remus stories. Many of the scattered tribes of the woodlands of eastern American had humorous stories about Rabbit, who tried to deceive the other animals. He cuts a road through a thicket where a race is to be run so that he can win against Deer. He steals Otter's coat. He escapes some Wolves by teaching them to dance.

Sometimes Rabbit is successful, other times not; sometimes he is very smart, often quite stupid. Still, the Cherokees understood his rascally ways and liked him.

This Rabbit is what folklorists call a trickster hero. And one thing is certain, he is always in trouble. Several of the Cherokee stories begin, "The Rabbit was the leader of them all in mischief."

The Cherokees liked Wiggan, just as they liked Rabbit in their folk tales. Eleazer Wiggan was their interpreter on many occasions when government officials toured through their towns. The Cherokees wanted him at their sides whenever they were ordered to Charles Town, for they trusted him entirely.

It happened that the Indian Board sent for a Cherokee to come and testify before them. He answered that he

wouldn't unless Wiggan would come to act as his interpreter.

The Board ordered the Old Rabbit there. He knew he
had the upper hand. He refused until the Board returned
some money it had taken from him a few months before,
unnecessarily, Wiggan thought. And not till the colonial
governor himself made the request and promised him his
money would the Old Rabbit make the trip to Charles
Town, bringing the wanted Cherokee with him.

When a group of seven Cherokees journeyed to England
in 1730 to visit, their official interpreter was Eleazer Wiggan. All had a fine time dining with King George II, going
to the Theatre-Royal to see two plays, and living at the
Mermaid Tavern.

Over the years trading varied as the colonial government tried different methods to regulate it. No system
seemed to work for the benefit of all interests. Yet neither
these legal curbs nor the physical hardships kept people
away. Instead, all kinds of men were attracted to the oc-
cupation.

Many who went into the Indian country were scheming
and unpleasant. John Elliott, the Scotchman of Chota, was
such a person. He cheated the Indians in the prices of
goods, and he used "false stilliards, short yards and little
measures." Others figured they were better than the red
men and tried to make servants of them. Or they abused
them frequently as did Phillip Gilliard, who cruelly whip-
ped a girl and her brother and made a woman drunk with
rum and locked her up from her mother, threatening to
kill them both when they protested the rough treatment.

There were those who were willing to help smooth the way for better Indian-white relations and were prompt to report troubles to colonial officials so that peace and trade could continue. Ludovick Grant was such a person, and his intelligence and sagacity were invaluable to the Carolina government. A great number always treated the Indians fairly. Samuel Benn, described by the Indians as "a very honest man," was one who did so, as was Anthony Deane, a learned Jesuit and a man of influence among the Overhill Cherokees.

However widely the traders differed in other ways, there was one thing most of them held in common—they all hoped to make money. Eleazer Wiggan had begun with such a goal, but when his get-rich-quick scheme with the Yuchi slaves failed, he was faced with a choice. Should he quit the trading business altogether? America was a land of opportunity. He could try many other occupations, any one of which might bring him riches galore. Or, on the other hand, should he stick to trading? He was shrewd enough to realize that if he did, he would never accumulate any great amount of money, but he would have a good livelihood. He chose to stick to trading.

Perhaps the fact that he liked the Indians and enjoyed trading with them made his decision easy. The carefree and lively life in their wilderness towns probably appealed greatly to him. The Indians' wild sense of humor matched his own impish nature. Whatever influenced him, the decision reached, Wiggan was a steady, honest trader. Twenty years he lived with the red men, mostly among the Cherokees. It might even have been for a longer time, for it is not known when he died. During his lifetime he made many Indian friends. And at his death the ghost of "the cheerful, inoffensive *old rabbet*" might have traveled westward to the "Darkening Land" to join the ghosts of his departed Cherokee friends and to await the arrival of other companions. The Indians would have wanted him with them in the spirit world surely.

Eleazer Wiggan made no fortune, but at least he was never overwhelmingly in debt to the merchants of Charles Town as a great majority of the other traders usually were. Sometimes it took a special act from the governor to allow a trader to enter Charles Town to transact official business. Otherwise, the man would have been seized at the request of some merchant and thrown into prison for his unpaid bills.

Actually, the traders deserved better treatment by the Colony of South Carolina, for it was they who had the task of keeping Indian nations on friendly terms with the English. Such Indian tribes were used as guards against the French along the colony's frontier. The lowly, simple white trader played a tremendous part in the English-French duel for the interior of America, which was to end finally in the French and Indian War.

The Old Rabbit was only one in a long list of Indian traders who lived a dangerous, adventurous life on the Western Waters. Some were good, some were bad, but all carried the white man's path a little farther into the wilderness.

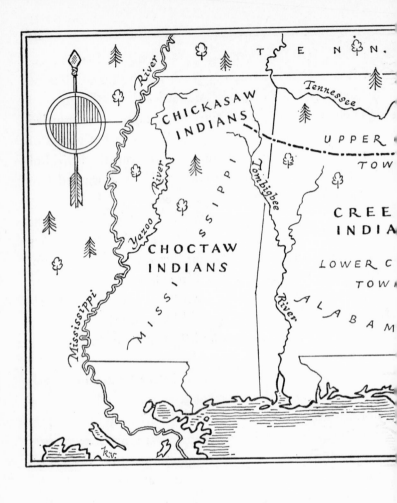

~ *Part Two* ~

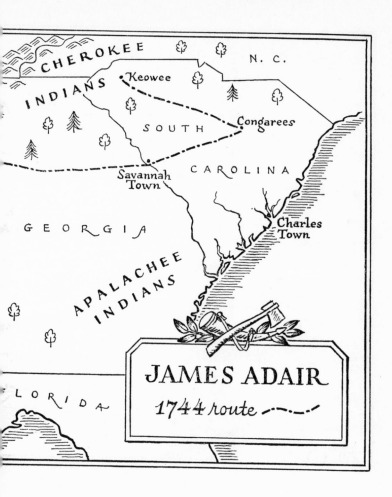

James Adair, author, and his search for the Lost
Tribes of Israel among the Indians in the 1740's.

1

"The Fragments of Ancient Days"

A riddle walked the American continent. James Adair had met it on the trails as he moved inland. It went before him through the low passes when he crossed to the far side of the mountains. Among the tall trees he had found the ashes of its campfire.

What was this riddle? It was the red men, the Indians. Where had they come from?

That was the riddle that intrigued trader James Adair as he passed through Keowee, a town of the Lower Cherokees. Most of the other traders didn't care where the Indians had originated. There they were, and, as far as was known, there in the forests of America the red man had always been. All that mattered to the traders was whether the Indians would buy their wares.

But James Adair was different from his fellow traders. Making money was not important to him. He had the kind of mind that asks and seeks and pokes and pries. It wasn't his nature to accept things as they appeared but always to inquire into the whys and wherefores. History, especially, seemed to him a fascinating thing. How had the peoples of the earth scattered to its four corners and become so different from one another?

At home in Northern Ireland, the young Adair had read

and studied and asked himself many questions. But scholar though he was, Adair was also a man of action. He had a fortune to seek and he knew where he wanted to seek it—in America, that new and strange and wonderful land whose very name stirred his curiosity.

So in 1735 he came to these shores and became an Indian trader, for Indians had always interested him. And shortly he found himself more and more interested. He liked Indians, brown and gentle people with a way of life so different from the white man's. And beyond that, there were all those unanswered questions: what was "the time and manner of seating this unknown world" and what kind of people were they before they became the many tribes of red men?

Adair walked along the street between the houses of Keowee. Though he had been trading with the Indians for eight years, today he stared at each one he met as if he had never before seen an Indian. Once again he noticed their small black eyes, their coarse hair, their prominent cheekbones. He was impressed, as always, at how Oriental-looking the Indians were.

And there the riddle began. Because they had the appearance of Asians, did it mean the Indians had come to America from that faraway continent? It was an argument that had much in its favor. Yet, how could it be proved?

Adair came to a house beside which stood a war pole. He paused to study it. The pole was a peeled sapling with the branches chopped off. At the top hung two scalps turning about in the breeze. The "speaking trophies of blood" had been tied onto hoops of cane with deer sinews. And both the hoops and the scalps were painted red, the color that stood for war.

In ancient times the Scythians on the Asian steppes had scalped their enemies. The American Indians did also. Could this possibly mean that the red men were descended from the Scythians? It was a most intriguing idea.

Adair moved on. In front of him walked a woman with her hair cropped close to her head. He knew why. It was a custom that whenever any Indian woman died, the female members of her family mourned for her for three months. At the end of this period all of them then cut off their long hair.

He had once read of this very same custom among the ancient Egyptians. Perhaps, then, the Indians came originally from Egypt? It was the riddle again and he could not answer it.

Yesterday he had listened to a Cherokee medicine man sing religious songs as he treated a sick warrior. This priest performed his cures in the same manner as Jewish Magi had in former times. Did that mean the Indians had once lived in the land of the Hebrews?

Of all the peoples of the world from whom the Indians might be descended, James Adair thought the Hebrews the most likely prospect. He had observed several Indian customs that were the same as those of the Jews. And it had made him wonder if the Indians might be the offspring of the Ten Lost Tribes of Israel.

Long ago when the Hebrews had been conquered at

Samaria in Israel and taken to Assyria as captives, ten of
the Jewish tribes disappeared. What had happened to
them? No one knew. They had just disappeared from history and were never mentioned again. Now what if the
Ten Tribes had wandered across Asia and finally ended
up here in America? It was a startling but magnificent
idea, and it made Adair's mind churn with vague thoughts
and half-answered questions.

For the moment he forgot he had to get these deerskins
and horses to the trading post called the Congarees, located where the Saluda joined the Congaree River. He
forgot that Thomas Brown and George Haig, his friends
and associates, wanted him to trade, not to find out the
answer to a riddle. However, he could think of nothing
but this new idea of his. He did not notice that he had left
Keowee or that splashing through creek after creek had
wet him to the skin. He followed the path, deep in
thought.

What was the best way to prove that the Indians were
descended from the Ten Lost Tribes? There were no
written records to study. The Indians themselves could
tell him little of their past history. But what if he closely
observed the red men's religious rites, their funeral ceremonies, their various manners and traditions, and all other
such "fragments of ancient days"? Then, item by item,
these could be compared with the Jewish rites and customs. If they were similar in a whole "variety of partic-
ulars," would this not prove their relationship? He felt it
most certainly would.

He suddenly realized that he was on the trail leading southeastward to the Congarees. There were still a good many miles to go. He jerked on the horses' lead line and hastened up the rise.

At the crest he stopped and looked off through the new green leaves of the trees to the distant mountains. Somewhere beyond those tumbled blue heaps of stone he would find the answer to his riddle. He breathed deeply. There was a wild sweet freshness to the spring air. He had never felt as fine as he did at this moment with a puzzle for his enquiring mind to try to solve.

James Adair turned and continued on the trail to the Congarees trading post.

2

The Mysterious Name for God

By the following autumn, 1744, James Adair had left the Congarees and was heading for that far-off frontier of British colonial trade, the Chickasaw settlements on the headwaters of the Tombigbee River. If he was still associated with Brown and Haig, then perhaps he went west to try to expand their trading operations. If he went on his own, he might have gone because competition was not as keen there as among tribes closer to the trading posts.

Whatever the reason, he must have rejoiced at the opportunity to go and live among the Chickasaws because he realized that there he had the best chance to try to prove his theory about the Indians' Jewish roots. The red men who were easily reached by the traders lost their old ways of living very quickly. Adair had observed that many tribes "have so exceedingly corrupted their primitive rites and customs" that there would not long be a possibility of tracing their origin.

At Savannah Town, Adair and his pack train took the old Chickasaw trading path. It was the route the first English traders from Charles Town had taken to the Chickasaws in the closing years of the seventeenth century. It wound westward among the foothills of the Southern Appalachians and across what was described on a contemporary map as a "Rich Oak and Hickery Land mixt with Pleasant Savanas."

He must have left early enough to avoid the heavy rains so common in the fall and early winter in these southern parts. There were many broad, deep streams to cross. And though the traders were "commonly hardy, and also of an amphibious nature," once it rained the creeks and rivers became unpassable to any but desperate people. Seldom would a trader risk his life or his trade goods crossing a stream in flood.

But if the streams were within their banks, then he got out his canoe of tanned leather. On each side the leather overlapped so that long saplings, freshly cut on the spot, could be inserted and slid into place from stem to stern. Other saplings were used for ribs and as a keel and were tied into place with deerskin strings. In half an hour a trader could "rig out a canoe, fit to carry over ten horse loads at once." It was a most ingenious and useful "apparatus," this instant canoe.

On Adair went, through town after town of the Upper Creek Indians, until, after seven weeks of hard travel, he reached the Chickasaw country. The French had been trying for some time to destroy this nation, so that by the time of Adair's arrival the remains of this once formidable people consisted of less than five hundred warriors. However the Chickasaws were terrible fighters, no matter what their number, and their name was as dreadful as it was hateful to the French.

James Adair immersed himself at once in the life of the Chickasaws. He made it clear that his intentions were the friendliest. He began to learn the language, and he watched closely everything that took place. He did not know yet what details he would use to try to convert his theory into the shape of real history, so he noted everything.

The Chickasaws went to the river to bathe often. Adair thought this frequent dipping in the water must be a religious duty with them and could therefore be termed truly Jewish. He noticed that every hunter who killed a deer cut a small piece out of the lower part of the haunch and threw it away. No one could tell why this was done. Adair thought that surely this custom must be derived from that of the children of Israel not eating the sinew of the thigh of any animal.

He noticed the many things the Indians ate. However, the Chickasaws would not eat meat that was "unclean," such as hogs and wolves, panthers, or rats and mice either. This certainly was a custom relating to the Jews, he felt. Adair was interested to see how the Indians hated moles and would never allow their children to touch one for fear the young ones would lose their eyesight and be blind like the mole.

Winter came, and the people retired to their hothouses. This was the time for visiting and for listening to tribal tales and history. Lying on the broad couches or beds through the long days and nights, Adair must have heard much that fascinated him and made him glad that he had come to live among these people.

With warmer weather Adair wandered about the town watching the Indian women prepare deerskins for making moccasins or thigh-length leggings. The skins were soaked in a puddle of water, and deer brains were rubbed into them. Then the skins were scraped to remove the hair. After that, they were smoked on both sides over a fire of rotten wood. This made the skins more durable, and no matter how often they were washed after that, as long as they were dried in the shade the skins never hardened but stayed soft and supple as chamois.

Once the white trader saw a medicine man bleed an ailing brave by "scratching the arms and legs with goirfish teeth." First, the skin had been "well loosened by warm water." There was another kind of scratcher besides that one made of gar teeth. The other was made of rattlesnake fangs fastened in a length of split cane. Sometimes an Indian was punished by being scratched with this comb-shaped instrument and without the privilege of warm water to soften the skin. This was called dry-scratching and was very painful. But a person scratched in this fashion gave no sign of the hurt, lest he be laughed at, not only for being wicked but also for lacking courage.

Adair was a good shot and often did his own hunting in the woods. One warm day he was returning with a haunch of venison. As he jogged along, he came suddenly upon a huge rattlesnake coiled in the middle of the path. It was live with motion, its neck waving back and forth ready to lunge at the white man. Its rattles whirred loudly. It hissed and flicked its tongue in and out of its open mouth. Adair dropped his meat and quickly raised his musket to shoot the snake.

A voice called for him to stop. The trader hesitated. The voice spoke again. The trader lowered his weapon and looked around. From the bushes stepped a Chickasaw archimagus, or high priest. His name was Pastabe.

The Indian told Adair not to shoot the rattlesnake, for it was the chief of the snake tribe. And if the white man killed it, the relatives of the rattler would not like that. They would send another snake to hunt for Adair. This snake would find the trader no matter where he was and would kill him in retaliation for slaying the rattlesnake.

Adair, like most white traders, hated rattlesnakes and usually killed them whenever possible. He pointed out to the old man how dangerous it was to have such a huge serpent so close to the town.

Pastabe very gravely answered that this snake was not

dangerous, that no rattler was anything but the kindest of creatures. A rattler would never bite a person unless that person disturbed it, the old man went on. Besides, it was a most thoughtful snake, for it used a bell to warn all where it was lying so it could be avoided.

Then the high priest took from a pouch several pieces of fern snakeroot. He chewed this up and spat the juice into his hands. Next, he rubbed this over his hands and arms. Advancing to the snake, he grabbed the thick body and picked it up. The snake twisted and coiled, but it did not bite him. He walked over to a hollow tree and very carefully placed the rattler inside.

The priest told Adair it would not bite him now. Nor would there be any need for the trader to kill it and so bring misfortune on himself. He gave the white man a piece of the root, saying that wild horehound or St. Andrew's cross were also good herbs to keep snakes away or to cure the "jarring qualities of the burning poison." He himself used Seneca, or fern snakeroot, because he thought it was the best.

Adair thanked the old man and invited him to come to his house and help eat the venison. The archimagus accepted. As they walked along toward the village, Adair told the Chickasaw a Cherokee tale.

He said that back in the Cherokee mountains between two lofty peaks there was a valley filled with old mossy rocks and big cedars and pines. In that place lived "some bright old inhabitants, or rattle snakes, of a more enormous size than is mentioned in history." Each of these snakes had a large jewel in its forehead. These carbuncles sent out piercing rays of light and were magical. The Cherokee conjurers used them to foretell all sorts of things.

Adair went on to say he knew a Cherokee prophet who had one of these carbuncles "near as big as an egg." And it sparkled with such brilliance as to light up his winter house like strong flashes of continued lightning. It was buried with the Cherokee prophet when he died.

The Chickasaw priest nodded his head. He had just such a stone, he assured Adair. He used his for making rain.

Adair asked to see it.

The old priest said he could not show his "divine stone." To do so would pollute it, and it would then no longer work. He begged the trader to forgive him for acting this way, but many nations had certain beloved things that were not meant for viewing by outsiders.

He went on to tell Adair how he fasted to be in great favor with the gods. Sometimes before attempting to bring rain, he would eat green tobacco leaves or drink a pot of hot button-snakeroot tea. Then he would spend several days by himself, listening to the quacking of the ducks or to the ravens croaking in the dead trees around his house. This told him much about the promise of rain. But when he was still doubtful, he would kill a bird and feel its feathers, for there was a certain moistness of the air in birds' quills.

Finally, when the priest felt the time was right, he would take his magic carbuncle from its hiding place. He would place it in a basin of water. After that he began his chanting, YO HE WAH, and so brought down the rain.

Adair could hardly believe his ears. Had the old priest really said YO HE WAH? That was actually Jehovah, "the favourite name of God, YO HE WAH, according to the ancient pronounciation." He was very excited. He would have to question the old priest more about this, for here was a beginning of his proof that the Indians were of Jewish origin.

3

The English Chickasaw

James Adair and Pastabe became great friends. Spring nights the priest came to the white trader's house. Lying on buffalo robes spread over the cane beds, they would talk late into the night till all was quiet in the village around them. Pastabe spoke of many things, of how to make turkey-feather blankets, of trading beyond the Mississippi River, of how the sun might possibly be as broad and round as his winter house but no bigger.

The trader always listened attentively, but he never missed an opportunity to turn the conversation toward his own interest. Did the Chickasaws use YO HE WAH in their religious ceremonies?

And the archimagus told him how when the black drink

was served at religious services in conch shells, the attendants always sang YO HE WAH; that most of the Chickasaw's religious dances began by the chanting of YO HE WAH, and it was repeated over and over as the dancers bowed and swayed.

Adair marveled that after all these centuries the Indians had retained the divine name of Jehovah, YO HE WAH. He asked more and more questions and the priest answered. And it seemed to the trader that even the Indian language had "the very idiom and genius" of the Hebrew tongue.

Still, Adair did not forget his manners. He saw to it that his guest had food if he was hungry. Often he made Pastabe a hot drink. He had brought in his pack train plenty of chocolate, coffee, and sugar, and the old priest enjoyed the sweet taste of these. At other times the two drank potions made of herbs the Indian collected from the woods. These native drinks came to have a special appeal to the white man. He noted especially that the early buds of sassafras and the leaves of ginseng make a most excellent tea, equally pleasant to the taste and conducive to health.

But nothing had as great an appeal as extracting information from Pastabe. As the weeks passed, Adair found out that the Indians had a holy place, which from the description the trader thought must be similar to the Jews' "sanctum sanctorum." And the Chickasaws had a holy fire as did the Israelites.

Pastabe went on to explain that when the holy fire was made for the yearly atonement of sin, the Indian priest dressed in white with a white buckskin tied around his shoulders. On the priest's feet were a new pair of buckskin white "maccasenes" made by the priest himself and sewed with sinew from the same animal.

That night, as soon as his visitor had left, Adair took out his Bible. He turned to Leviticus and read how Aaron went into the holy place, how Aaron dressed in white linen clothes. The trader closed the book and gazed into the dying fire on the clay hearth in the center of his house. Here was another example to add to the long list of Indian customs that were the same as those of the Jews.

There was no longer any doubt in his mind. He had solved the riddle that walked the American continent. But he would not stop there. He would collect as much evidence as he could. Who knew? Perhaps some day he would write an essay about this and give the "Literati proper and good materials for tracing the origin of the American Indians."

With warmer weather there was much activity in the Chickasaw town. Adair took part in everything. He went to the meetings in the council house. He helped erect the picket palisade that surrounded the town. He went to the ball games played between towns. Once he even attended a funeral and saw that the Indians were as careful in the burial of their dead as had been the ancient Hebrews. And, of course, he carried on his business of trading.

Now, Adair began to dress as the Chickasaw men did. He knew the Indians affixed the idea of helplessness and effeminacy to the wearing of breeches. It was a "pinching custom" they did not care to follow. Adair wore their breechclout, "a slip of cloth, about a quarter of an ell wide, and an ell and an half long, in lieu of breeches."

This flap was made of one piece of soft deerskin about five and a half feet long by a foot wide. It was passed between the legs and over a belt at the waist so that the ends of it hung loose in the front and at the rear. Or the ends could be tucked under the belt.

In a breechclout and barefooted, Adair padded around the town with the other men. But if they went hunting, then they added to this costume a pair of leggings, or thin deerskin boots, well smoked, that reached high up their thighs. This protected their legs from "the brambles and braky thickets." They also put on moccasins made from bear and elk skins. These were well dressed and smoked to prevent hardening.

Talking as a native American and dressed in their clothes, James Adair, the white trader, became truly an "English Chickasaw." He was accepted as one of the tribe. Still, there was one more thing Adair had to do. He had to pick up the war hatchet and prove himself a man and a warrior, for this was the highest praise the Chickasaws could bestow on any mortal.

Could he do it?

4

"A Long Train of Crying Blood"

The morning light slanted across the village. Children played with the dogs in the shadows before the houses. A woman slapped and pounded a pile of clay, which she would soon shape into a pot. Seated on a skin in the sun was an old man, carving a piece of soft soapstone into a pipe.

The July sunlight came through the open doorway and lay in a yellow square on the dirt floor of James Adair's summer house. The trader sat on a cane stool reading. Flies buzzed about him. A small silver-gray butterfly paused for a moment, wings folded, on the top of his book, then whirled away.

Suddenly a shrill whoop sounded. Adair jumped to his feet and ran to the door. Two houses away a warrior was beginning to circle his house, beating on a drum and chanting a war song. It was Payah Matahah. He was calling for volunteers to go with him to avenge his brother recently killed by the Choctaws.

This was the chance James Adair had been wanting. He would go. Payah Matahah was his friend and would not refuse to take him. He slipped his shot pouch and powder-horn straps over his head. Taking a bag of parched corn, he left his house with his rifle, knife, and tomahawk, ready to go on the warpath.

Adair joined those standing by the winter house listening to the Chickasaw warrior's chant. Payah Matahah passed from the west side of the small house to the east side. At the end of the third time around, he stopped before the crowd and began to speak in a deep, commanding voice, very fast with only an occasional pause.

He told the group that the Choctaws had killed his brother, that last month the same cowardly enemy had murdered several of his kin. Now the blood of his own flesh and bone was crying out for revenge. He wanted all those warriors who were not afraid to leave the white path of peace to come with him on the red warpath, to come with him to revenge "a long train of crying blood."

As Adair listened, he thought of that law of Moses that said, "He who sheddeth man's blood, by man shall his blood be shed." He knew that not only Chickasaws but all Indians believed in revenging any wrong done to one of them or to their families. They could never rest till they had retaliated and righted the wrong.

Payah Matahah cried that he knew the guns were burning in the hands of the warriors before him, that he felt their tomahawks were thirsty and ready to drink the blood of the Choctaws, and that he could tell their arrows were impatient to be on the wing. He did not want delay to eat away their hearts. He asked them to come with him and be sanctified for battle.

He gave an ear-splitting war cry. Turning, he led the way to the entrance of his hothouse and entered, chanting. Adair and a dozen Chickasaws followed him inside. Payah

Matahah welcomed them. He was especially happy to see the "English Chickasaw."

The group stayed in the winter house for three days and nights. No one was allowed to come inside, for this was a time of religious fasting. The war leader watched closely to see that no one ate secretly or slipped from the house at night. All the while they drank a hot concoction "highly imbittered with button-rattle-snake-root." This was to purify each of them and so take them safely through the coming dangers. At regular intervals Payah Matahah sprinkled them with this same holy water.

The war captain picked from the group a great warrior to be the "Hettisu, or beloved waiter." Everything the war party ate or drank during the journey must come from the waiter's sacred hands.

When the fasting and purification were completed, the war leader strapped the holy ark on his back. This was a covered square container woven from thin hickory splints. Inside were sacred vessels "of such various antiquated forms, as would have puzzled Adam to have given significant names to each."

Then they left the town with much whooping and shouting and shooting of their guns. Payah Matahah went at the front with the ark, singing a solemn song. Behind him walked the waiter, then the other men, three or four steps' distance from each other.

Adair, his body as brown as the Indian's, in breechclout and moccasins, was in the middle of the single file. He sounded the "war whoo-whoop" every few steps as did the others in the line.

The moment the group reached the woods beyond the town they became silent. At a fast trot they traveled southward toward Choctaw country. By midmorning Adair was so weak from lack of food, he could hardly keep up with the others. He did not dare eat his parched corn, nor drink from any stream they crossed, for that would ruin the "divine favour" and bring failure to the war party.

Nor could he so much as lean against a tree when a rest was called by the leader. Sitting was prohibited, too. Adair found this almost more than he could bear, but he was determined to follow the Indians' war customs. And he kept gamely on.

The sacred ark was not allowed to touch the ground. It was placed on rocks or short logs at each rest. When the war leader tired, the waiter carried the ark. So the war party kept up a steady pace all the first day. That night when they halted, the waiter gave each man a sip of water and a small amount to eat.

Adair had such hunger pains that it was hard to get to sleep. And when he did, he had terrible dreams. He did not mention these dreams, however, for fear the warriors would construe them as an evil omen and send him back to the village.

By the middle of the second day, they came upon the tracks of the enemy. Payah Matahah scouted ahead. On returning, he told them he had seen ten Choctaws heavily laden with meat and traveling slowly. Excitement went through the standing line of warriors. This offered them a good chance for their favorite mode of fighting—ambuscade. The Chickasaws began to paint their faces and breasts red as blood, intermingled with black streaks. Adair did the same thing.

Now the hickory bows were strung, the guns checked. Adair loosened the tomahawk in the thong at his belt. He twisted the strap from which hung his long-pointed knife, so that the sheath rested on his breast, where he could reach it quickly. He was tense and expectant. Still, he would feel more like fighting if he had some water to drink.

The waiter stayed behind to guard the holy ark. Payah Matahah led the others away from the path and off through the woods. When they were close to the Choctaws, the war party spread out and surrounded their enemy. Now they moved in closer and closer, "by their wild-cat-method of crawling."

Adair, too, moved forward on his stomach, sliding his gun cautiously ahead of him. Suddenly Payah Matahah blew his whistle. The attack began and Adair was never to forget his first battle:

"The guns are firing; the chewed bullets flying; the strong hiccory bows a twanging; the dangerous barbed arrows whizzing as they fly; the sure-shafted javelin striking death wherever it reaches; and the well-aimed tomohawk killing or disabling its enemy. Nothing scarcely can be heard for the shrill echoing noise of the war and death-whoop, every one furiously pursues his adversary from tree to tree. . . . One dying foe is intangled in the hateful and faltering arms of another: and each party desperately attempts both to save their dead and wounded from being scalped, and to gain the scalps of their opponents. . . . Now they retreat: then they draw up into various figures, still having their dead and wounded under their eye. Now they are flat on the ground loading their pieces—then they are up firing behind trees, and immediately spring off in an oblique course to recruit—and thus they act till winged victory declares itself."

By the time the fight ended, most of the Choctaws had escaped into a swamp. Payah Matahah would not allow his warriors to chase after the enemy. He knew if he lost several braves in the swamp, his drum, war whistle, and possibly even his war title, earned in previous battles, would be taken from him. Then he would have to use his boy's name till he had earned himself a new title in battle.

There were three dead Choctaws and these were scalped. The scalps were put on hoops to preserve them and then were painted red. Payah Matahah's "crying blood" had been revenged with these.

Adair was pleased that he had fought as well as he had, considering how weak he was from lack of food and water. However, the next time he came on a war party, he planned to take water in a large hollow cane well corked at each end. He would "sheer off now and then to drink" and eat a bite without the others knowing it.

Now the war party returned home. A runner was sent ahead with news of the victory and with the order that the winter house be made clean and ready for them, for they must fast and purify themselves once again.

The line of warriors entered the village singing the

death song. Every now and then one of them would sound "the shrill death Whoo Whoop Whoop." The scalps were carried on small branches of pine. They were placed on the winter-house roofs of Payah Matahah's relations to show that their deaths had finally been revenged.

After the purification there would be a victory dance in which the battle would be re-enacted for the onlooking town people. James Adair would take part in this too, for he had earned the respect of his Chickasaw neighbors.

5

The Rusticated Author

The Chickasaws accepted James Adair as a friend and brother and as an honest trader. But they were so suspicious of him as an author that he was forced to keep his papers hidden from them while writing. The Indians had received from white colonial officials many letters filled with promises, few of which had ever been fulfilled. As a result, all writing became "lying black marks" to them.

The distrustful Indians were only a part of Adair's troubles. His business of trading kept him from his writing for long periods at a time. There was no library in which he could seek the factual information he needed. And in order to be accurate in his comparisons of the Jewish customs with those of the red men, he had to teach himself Hebrew.

Still, he had a "genius naturally formed for curious enquiries," and none of the difficulties stopped him from writing his book, not even the fact that he was "Rusticated by 30 years residence in a Wild Country." When at last it was finished, he took it himself to London, and there *The History of the American Indians* was published in 1775.

In the book the author gave twenty-three arguments to prove that the Indians were descended from the Jews. He could have listed many more, he pointed out, but he did not want to seem tedious. The examples he gave only made many readers jeer at his theory and consider it eccentric. Today, it is known that there are numerous points of likeness among primitive peoples but that Indians did not descend from the Hebrews. Back in Adair's time, however, many ministers, historians, and writers were concerned about such a possibility and sought evidence to support it. James Adair was, in fact, only one of a long list of such people who wrote on the subject.

Of all these many books, Adair's has proven to be the most useful. He "sat down to draw the Indians on the spot," and the result was a valuable record of the customs of the southern Indians before the white men entirely changed their primitive way of life. There was much in the book, too, of colonial history, of the bickerings of government officials, and of the abuses of traders, but information about the author was scarce. Only the most meager details turn up about himself or about such adventures as his exploits on the warpath or of his capture and escape from the French. If he mentioned a dangerous situation in which he was involved, he dismissed it casually with "my usual good fortune enabled me to leave them far enough behind."

In his book there is this statement: "When an Indian and a trader contract friendship, they exchange the clothes then upon them, and afterwards they cherish it by mutual presents, and in general, will maintain it to the death." James Adair gave the Chickasaws his clothes and took theirs and made friends with a whole nation, "the cheerful brave Chikkasah." He treated them as human beings, he fought their battles with their tomahawk, he traveled to Charles Town innumerable times to keep rum out of their nation and to ask for better trade regulations. And in breechclout and moccasins he wrote his Indian history, a final gift in his contracted and cherished friendship with them.

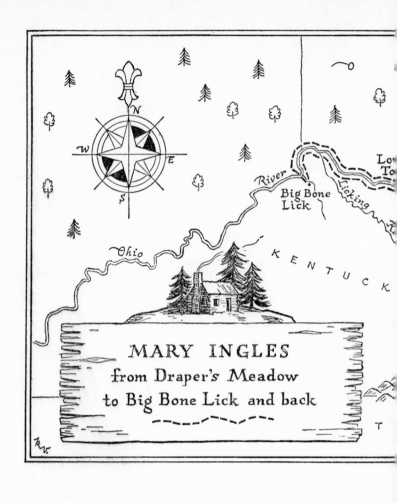

MARY INGLES
from Draper's Meadow
to Big Bone Lick and back

~ *Part Three* ~

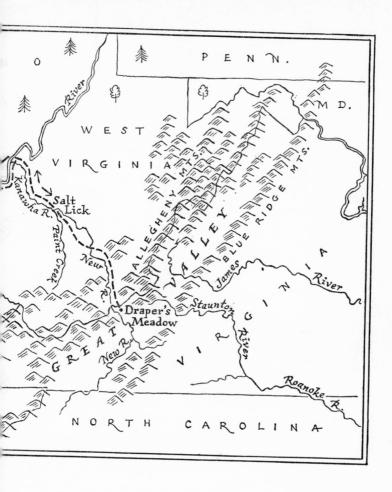

Mary Ingles, farmer's wife and Indian captive,
and her extraordinary adventures on the Western
Waters in 1755.

1

"A Further Dismal Account of Murders"

The settlement at Draper's Meadow in the back country of Virginia was different, though perhaps a casual observer might not have been able to distinguish this farming community from others like it in the Great Valley. The cabins were of round logs, notched at the corner, chinked in between. There were cowsheds and corncribs and a mill along one of the creeks. Wheat ripened in some fields and corn was "in the milk" in others. Cows stood in the shade of huge oaks in the meadows. Pigs soused themselves in the mud around the springs or sniffed through the rail fence at the vegetables in the "truck patch" gardens. The difference wasn't in any of these things.

What was it that made Draper's Meadow different? It was the river. Not the mudbanks where the turtles sunned, nor the stretches of quiet water ending in sand bars. These were common features of all rivers in the Great Valley between the Blue Ridge and the Allegheny Mountains. It was the direction in which this river flowed that made the difference. Other rivers in the valley along which settlers lived went north or east and ended up in the Atlantic Ocean. New River flowed to the west, the first such one that the pioneers found in the Great Valley.

Thus, Draper's Meadow on the New River was the first settlement in Virginia on the Western Waters. Perhaps it has mattered more to historians that here was a "first" than it did to John Draper and William Ingles, who began the settlement in 1748. These two would have known that New River flowed into the Ohio River and not the South Sea as Virginians three-quarters of a century before had believed. They would have known, but probably they wouldn't have cared. They were interested in land, not geography. They were two of numberless industrious, frugal farmers moving slowly but steadily toward the interior of the continent. They wanted fertile land to cultivate, not historical "firsts."

The two farmers did well at Draper's Meadow. Their herds and their acreage increased yearly. In time William Ingles married John Draper's sister, Mary. This provided another first for historians—the first marriage of British subjects to take place on the Western Waters.

Probably Mary Ingles was not even conscious of this, and it may be she would not have cared if she had known. She did care about a home, and at Draper's Meadow she had found one. She had moved often before coming here. Now she was settled. Here in the valley with the mountains around she would raise her family. How comforting to stay in one spot, to look up, day after day, and find the same mountains, friendly and peaceful on the horizon. This was as far west as she wanted to travel ever.

Mrs. Ingles must have been well satisfied with her life in Draper's Meadow. The crops and animals prospered.

The Ingleses had a warm, snug cabin. Mary had two children, Thomas, age four, and George, two. And another child was expected soon.

That July morning of 1755 she had a visitor, a friend who had helped her husband and her brother to begin this settlement. It was Colonel James Patton. Since he had helped the two Irish boys, he had taken a lively interest in all their activities and visited them whenever he could spare the time.

Colonel Patton had arrived at Draper's Meadow with a supply of lead and powder. He was in charge of the militia in that region, and he wanted this frontier outpost to be prepared for trouble and to resist it if it came. The French were stirring up the northern Indians, and there had already been raids at other border settlements.

The governor of the colony, Robert Dinwiddie, was worried about the back country people and had written to Patton: "I am sorry to hear a further dismal account of murders. . . . I fear your people are seized with panic in suffering the Indians in such small companies to do the mischief they do without raising to oppose them." So Patton was encouraging all settlers to stand firm.

The Great Indian War Path ran down the Great Valley of Virginia. Not far from where the Ingles cabin stood, a trail, which followed the New River to the red men's towns beyond the Ohio River, joined the Great War Path. And though Indians passed often back and forth over these paths, Draper's Meadow had never been molested. John Draper and William Ingles thought so little of Colonel

Patton's warning that they went to the wheat field that day to work as they always went—unarmed.

Colonel Patton sat writing at the puncheon table in the Ingles cabin. Before him were paper, quills, and an inkhorn. And there, too, on the table top lay the colonel's broadsword. He kept it with him at all times. Perhaps it was a habit he had acquired when serving in the British Royal Navy or else when he was captain of a ship that brought redemptioners from England to Virginia.

Mary Ingles sat in the yard near her cabin, watching her children play with the dogs. Several fields away, Mary's sister-in-law left her cabin to get an armload of wood. She noticed Indians slipping from the thicket and coming her way. They were painted in red and black. A war party! Colonel Patton had been right. She dashed inside and got her small baby from its crib. Then she fled.

The Shawnees saw her, and one raised his rifle and fired. The shot broke Mrs. Draper's arm. She dropped the child, but picked it up with her good arm and hurried on again. She did not get far before she was surrounded. The baby was taken from her and flung against a shed wall.

Mary Ingles did not even get a chance to run. The Shawnees captured her and her two boys without warning. In all the settlement, only Colonel Patton fought for his life. When two Indians rushed through the open door, the colonel sprang to his feet with his sword and hacked them to death. A third savage shot him dead from the doorway.

The cattle and pigs were slaughtered and left lying where they fell. All the cabins and sheds were burned. The powder and lead that the colonel had brought was shared among the raiders, as were the horses. A few of the other inhabitants were taken captive, the rest killed. Unarmed, John Draper and William Ingles—when they found they could do nothing—had no choice but to hide until the large party of Indians left. Then they rushed for help, but it did no good. The Shawnees had gone before horsemen could be rounded up. Mary's beloved Draper's Meadow was wiped out.

Colonel Patton, who had hoped to stiffen the resistance of the Great Valley settlers, only succeeded by his death in adding to their panic. About the same time General Braddock and his British army were defeated in western Pennsylvania. The French and Indian War had begun in earnest. Frontier settlers fled back across the Blue Ridge to the safety of towns where they had formerly lived.

In August, on hearing of Patton's death for the first time, Governor Dinwiddie wrote from his safe capital that he could not conceive what Patton had intended to do with ammunition "so far from the inhabited part of the country." He felt the colonel "was wrong to go so far back without a proper guard."

As he was writing this, Mary Ingles was going even farther back on the Western Waters. She was headed to where no white woman had ever been, another "first" to add to her list.

2

Salt from the Graveyard

At the edge of the settlement, miles from the Ingles cabin, the Shawnees added one last grisly touch to their massacre of Draper's Meadow. They cut off a man's head and placed it in a sack. Taking this to a neighboring cabin, they gave it to the woman who lived there and instructed her to look inside the bag and she would find an acquaintance.

Then the war party took the trail that led northward through the Allegheny Mountains and along New River. Mrs. Draper's arm hurt terribly, and her sister-in-law asked the Shawnees to help her. The group stopped, and one of the Indians led Mrs. Ingles to a meadow, where he showed her a wild comfrey plant and told her to search for others and gather the leaves. Under his directions, she boiled the leaves and mixed them with deer fat to make an ointment for the broken arm.

Wild comfrey became another simple to add to the pioneer's long list of "yarb and root" remedies learned from the Indians. It was given other names of bruisewort and healing herb and was much used for the relief of aches and pains along the frontier.

The Shawnees were willing to stop any time Mrs. Ingles wanted to gather comfrey. And the third day of travel they halted long enough for Mrs. Ingles to have her child. Then she and the baby girl were placed on a horse and the party kept going.

When the Shawnees reached the mouth of Paint Creek, they paused and stripped an elm of its bark. Then, on the white wood, one of the braves painted symbols so that all who passed might read of this successful raid on Draper's Meadow, for this was an Indian custom, to have such a record of scalps and prisoners taken on a raid, of the names of leaders and the number of dead and wounded warriors. There were other such trees here, and this had named the creek.

They had now reached the lower portion of the stream, but it was no longer called New River. It was known then as the Kanawha River, and it still is. There were many different ways of spelling it: Canais, Canaways, Canawese, Conhaway. However, these names all referred to the Conoy Indians, who had once lived here. They belonged to the Algonquin tribe, which had been driven away long ago. Only their name was left to recall that this had been their former home.

The war party crossed to the north side of the Kanawha, where there was a salt spring. They stayed there long enough for the captives to make a small quantity of salt in their own pots and kettles for the Indians. Moving on down the Kanawha Valley, they reached the Ohio River. They crossed it and proceeded downstream to one of the main towns of the Shawnees. Located at the mouth of the Scioto River, it was called Lowertown by most, though a few white traders knew it as Shannoah Town. Here in the center of the village was a "kind of State-House about 90 feet long, with a light cover of Bark in wch. they hold their councils."

At Lowertown the white captives were forced to run the gauntlet. Women, children, warriors—all who wanted to take part in the ceremony—grabbed sticks, stones, tomahawks, deer antlers, anything that would maim and hurt. They lined up in two rows. As the prisoners ran between them, the Indians tried to hit them as often as possible. White people found the gauntlet a terrifying experience, but the Indians thought it great fun. As one warrior explained it, the gauntlet was "a sort of how do do."

Mary Ingles was the only one who did not have to run the gauntlet. Why, she never found out, but she was glad to be spared. However, she was not spared the ordeal of having her sons taken from her. At Lowertown the war party broke up, and the braves scattered with their plunder and their prisoners to their own villages. Four-year-old Thomas Ingles went north to a town near Detroit, while his younger brother went to an unknown place. Mrs. Draper was taken to Chillicothe to be adopted by an Indian chief who had recently lost a daughter.

Mrs. Ingles and her baby girl remained in Lowertown. She was not mistreated, but she was forced to do heavy work. When the Shawnees discovered she could sew, she did no more heavy work but was kept busy with her needle. Two Frenchmen had arrived in the town with a quantity of checkered cloth to trade. The Shawnee braves bought the material and set Mrs. Ingles to work making shirts. Each time a garment was finished, the Indian owner would place it on a pole, and holding it over his head, he would run back and forth among the huts to show it off, all the time singing the praises of the white woman. And when at last he put it on, he would wear it with many airs and graces and much strutting and high stepping.

After weeks of shirtmaking, Mrs. Ingles and her baby were taken by boat down the Ohio River to Big Bone Lick in Kentucky. This was one of many places where the Indians made their salt. An old Dutch woman, captured by the Shawnees years before in Pennsylvania, went along to help with the work too.

The saltmakers left their boats and carried their pots through a ring of low hills into the valley, where the many springs of Big Bone Lick were located. The ground here had been torn up by the animals that came to drink the salt and sulphur waters and to wallow in the mud. There was no underbrush. There was a buffalo road five or six feet lower than the land around it and "beaten spacious enough for a wagon to go abreast, and leading straight to the Lick." The saltmakers took it to reach the springs.

The place was a marvel to see. Great skulls and tusks of prehistoric mammals lay half buried in the mud. Shoulder blades and hip bones of mastodons stuck up out of the dark sulphur pools. Bleached ribs and leg bones and vertabrae were in heaps and piles, while elephant teeth dotted the marshy ground.

Big Bone Lick impressed most who saw it. But only the

Indians had a story explaining how these springs had become a graveyard. One Indian chief told that the deer, elk, bear, and buffalo, which were created for the use of the Indians, came here to drink. The big animals did not like such small creatures to have these excellent springs, so they drove them away and took the lick for their own use. The Great Man above grew angry, seized his lightning, and descended to the earth. He sat on a mountain and hurled his fiery bolts at the big animals and killed all but one. It shook off the lightning and escaped to the north. Any who doubted this story could look on the mountain top and see where the Great Man sat and the print of his feet in the rock.

It is doubtful if the white women had time to view the curiosities of Big Bone Lick or to sit around and listen to any stories the Shawnees might have told. There was much work connected with saltmaking. The pots and kettles had to be kept filled with the salty water and the fires under them burning constantly. As the water boiled down, a mixture of salt, iodine, and other minerals was left in the bottom of the container. This was then put into sacks, and the work began all over. As a rule, it took about a thousand gallons of water to make a bushel of salt.

At times the women were sent into the woods to gather nuts and wild grapes for the Indians to eat. As neither one was watched on these sorties, Mrs. Ingles wondered if escape was possible. She discussed this with the Dutch woman, but the old woman scoffed at the idea.

The Dutch woman said that men seldom escaped from

the Shawnees and never women. Once she had seen a woman try it, and the Indians caught her and "beat her flat on her Face on the Ground; they then stuck her several Times, through the Back with a dart, to the Heart, scalped Her, and threw the Scalp in the Air, and another cut off her Head: there the dismal spectacle lay till the Evening."

The old woman then pointed out that if Mrs. Ingles got away from the Indians, she would likely get lost in the wilderness trying to reach Virginia. As for herself, she would rather stay alive and well fed as a Shawnee captive.

Mary Ingles paid no attention to this talk. She knew what a risk it was to travel through the mountains. Still, she was willing to attempt it. Draper's Meadow was where she longed to be. If William was alive, they could begin all over with their farm. If he was dead, at least her two boys were alive. She could ransom them from the Indians and her sister-in-law, too. The four of them could rebuild the settlement on New River if they were the only ones living. She would never be happy among the savages, far away from the Great Valley of Virginia. She would never be happy away from her own people, a slave to the Indians. It would be better to die trying to reach her home than not to make the effort at all.

When Mrs. Ingles made the decision to escape, she was faced with another one—what to do about her three-month-old baby girl. Should she take the child with her when she left? If she did and it cried, pursuers would find her or her hiding place easily. If she took it and got away from the Shawnees, would she have strength enough to carry it mile after mile through the bushes and over the rivers and mountains in all kinds of weather? Still, it was more than she could stand to think of leaving the baby, her first and only daughter, here among the savages.

What should she do?

As the days passed, she tried to make up her mind. While filling the pots with salt water, while chopping wood for the fires, while cooking for the braves, she went over and over her problem. At nights she lay awake pondering. But the saltmaking was almost completed. She had to decide. Any day the Shawnees would go back to their town at the mouth of the Scioto. Then it would be much more difficult for her to try to escape.

One morning she decided the time had come to leave. She told the Dutch woman. To keep from getting lost, she planned to follow the Ohio River to where the Kanawha entered it. She felt sure she could recognize the stream. Following the Kanawha, then the New River, she could get through the mountains and back to Draper's Meadow. It was a simple plan, but it was useless unless they could outdistance those who chased them. Could they elude the Shawnees? The Dutch woman decided they could and that she would come with Mrs. Ingles.

That afternoon the two women left the camp. Each had a blanket and a hatchet. And Mary Ingles—did she have the baby as well?

3

La Belle Rivière

The October afternoon was warm. The sun shone from a
bright metallic sky. The air was hazy, and the distant
hills around Big Bone Lick were a shapeless blue. The
Shawnees ate buffalo and strips of deer meat and talked.
On one side of the camp several gambled at a stick and
dice game.

But where were the white captives? They were seen
leaving camp with blankets in which to bring back grapes.
After a while, a couple of warriors strolled away in that
direction to look for them. It was most Indians' belief that
white women were easily lost in the woods. Back among
the trees the two Shawnees shouted and whooped. They
fired their guns a few times. There was no answering call.
Night was coming, so the Indians returned to camp, be-
lieving that the women had been destroyed by wild beasts.
The braves gave no further concern to them.

When the rifles sounded, Mrs. Ingles and the Dutch
woman were miles away in the opposite direction. They
had reversed their course when out of sight of the camp.
Now they jogged along, using the Ohio River to guide
them eastward. As they hurried through the trees, Mary
looked back over her shoulder often, fearful of sighting
the Shawnees. Twilight came, and still no one seemed to

be on their trail. The river gleamed like a silver thread on their left. They stayed back from its edge but kept it in sight.

Now it was dark, and they were forced to slow to a walk and feel their way. They kept moving, though. They did not want to stop so soon. They were still too close to Big Bone Lick. Perhaps, too, Mary Ingles wanted to go on till she was so bone-weary that she would go straight to sleep when they did halt. She did not want to lie awake and think about what she had done, for she had left her baby girl with the Shawnees. The decision had been a hard one for her, but it had been made and was over. From now on she would put all her thoughts and efforts into surviving. She must get home to Draper's Meadow.

At last, tired and wheezing painfully, the two women halted. They raked together a pile of leaves, rolled up in their blankets, and went to sleep. The next day would surely bring pursuit, for Mary couldn't believe they had escaped this easily.

By dawn they were up and hurrying toward the east once again. All that day they kept going, walking where the way was rough, trotting in the more open spaces. The old woman wanted to rest often, but Mary wouldn't let her. She kept the Dutch woman on her feet and moving. Every step brought them closer to freedom and to home. By late afternoon Mary felt relieved. They were not being followed by the Shawnees. She called a halt at the first spring, and they rested and washed themselves.

The third morning they moved on at a more leisurely pace, following the twists and bends of the Ohio. Though happy at their good fortune, it is doubtful if they felt cheerful enough to notice their surroundings. The French explorers had found no river to compare with the Ohio, and they called it "La Belle Rivière," the beautiful river. A flatboard traveler wrote that the river's "peculiarity is that it is *all* beautiful. There are no points bare of beauty."

Struggling along the banks, Mary Ingles must have had a different idea about the lush vegetation and thick forest that bordered the river. Along the Ohio there was a luxuriant growth of cane, which sometimes extended for miles in "brakes" and was so thick a man on horseback could hide himself without dismounting. It indicated rich land for farming and made fine scenery, but it was dangerous walking. The white women had to go around these places.

And the river bottoms, where the white bark of the sycamore stood out in ghostly rows, were low and sodden. Here the mud would suck at a traveler's feet and make walking slow and difficult. There were "hills pinching close on the river." These, too, they detoured around.

Of course, where the forests were old and the trees huge, there was little underbrush and good time could be made. However, such woods made it difficult to keep off a particular, unpleasant, anxious feeling caused by the continuing shadow and the confined outlook. Also unless a traveler had a good sense of direction, it was easy to get lost among the giant trunks and circle about for hours on end.

Mrs. Ingles stuck to the course of the Ohio, picking a way as best she could. The Dutch woman's strength began to give out, and there were frequent stops for rest. There was not enough time to search for the fruits and nuts that the Kentucky autumn woods provided, so they traveled often with empty stomachs.

Whenever the two women chanced upon an open space, there would be grape vines spreading over the bushes and climbing up into the low trees at the edge of the forest. In October they were loaded with grapes. At such spots the two ate all they could find of the sweet purple muscadines or the smaller, tart fox grapes. And when they reached a grove of hickories, chestnuts, or a stand of walnut trees, they would halt and crack the fallen nuts with their hatchets and make their meal on the meats inside.

Persimmon trees could be passed by. Their fruits would most likely be green this early in October and would not be eatable till after a frost or two. But the black wrinkled pawpaws were hanging on slender branches. Though they look unappetizing, the soft yellowish pulp of the fruit is very tasty and sweet.

Fruits and nuts—those were the women's steady diet. There were quite a lot of things available for eating: berries, such as haw or pipsissewa; roots from Indian cucumbers or from cattails; the inner bark of many trees. The list of emergency foodstuffs is long. But Mary Ingles was a farmer's wife, more familiar with garden "sass" and products from plowed fields than with what grew wild in the woods for eating raw. Often the two ravenous women must have passed by foodstuff in plenty without knowing it.

When the chance came to eat corn, the women were overjoyed. They had arrived at a cabin with a cornfield beyond it. There seemed to be no one living there, but Mary was cautious. Across the Ohio the smoke rose from the many huts of Lowertown. To have walked so far and to be recaptured now opposite their former Shawnee home was unthinkable. They hid in the bushes at the edge of the cabin's clearing.

For a little time they waited patiently. At last they could stand it no longer. The sight of the corn made their mouths water. And the chance to sleep indoors once again and cook on a hearth added to their restlessness. They crept across the open space and up to the door. It was ajar. Mary Ingles stepped up on the threshold, took another step forward, and was inside. The Dutch woman crowded up close behind her.

There was a movement in one corner. They turned in horror, too weak to run.

4

Dutch Hunger

A raccoon crouched in the corner, blinking indignantly at the intruders. With a last glance around the empty cabin, it padded calmly past them and out into the twilight.

Mary Ingles leaned against the door in relief. She had taken a greater risk than she should have. A warrior might have been sleeping in the cabin or a renegade white man who would have been delighted to take such female merchandise across the river to Lowertown. But she had slept on the ground so many nights, shivering with cold, that the opportunity to be indoors and perhaps have a fire and cook some ears of corn had made her act hastily. She should have waited till it was quite dark before coming to the cabin. However, it had turned out all right.

She sent the old woman out to gather corn while she searched the cabin. She found a piece of broken steel and a rifle flint, but little else. She did not mind. They would have a fire, and the darkness would hide the smoke. She did not believe the owner of the dwelling would come back tonight. From the dust inside, he seemed to have been gone for some time, and certainly he had taken all his possessions with him.

With the flat sides of their tomahawks the two beat the shelled grains of corn into meal on the hearth. This was mixed with water and set to baking on slanting stones by the fire. It would have been better with salt, but at least it was food that would "stick to their ribs." It would nourish them as fruit and nuts never had.

Their good luck lasted through the next morning. They had not gone far from the cabin when they found a horse with a bell around its neck. They tied their blankets filled with shelled corn on its back and took turns riding along the Ohio. Mary Ingles muffled the bell clapper with a piece of her skirt.

Now they made much better time. The only thing that slowed them was finding a place to ford the many rivers and deep creeks. Neither could swim, and they were scared to try a crossing on the horse's back. So they were forced to go miles upstream from a river's mouth to find a shallow place to wade across. Often this meant wasting as much as half a day's traveling time.

One day the women came to a river and, as usual, went along its course seeking a sand bar or a shoal. Not far from where the river joined the Ohio, they found a lodgement of drift wood, extending clear across the stream. Here was a fine place for them to cross. But what would they do with the horse? If they let it swim over, they might not catch it again.

The Dutch woman said the mat of logs would hold the animal. Mrs. Ingles did not think so. They argued for some time. At last the old woman got mad and led the horse down the bank and out onto the driftwood before Mary could stop her. All went well at first. About halfway across, however, the horse's feet slipped from a log. It ended up with its body across the log and its legs hanging down in the water on each side of it.

They struggled to get the beast off the log, but it was impossible. There was nothing to do but leave it in this position and go on. The Dutch woman took the bell. They crossed over the rest of the way and went back to the Ohio River to continue their way.

Now the old woman became discouraged. She fussed all the time, complaining that she was too hungry to walk any further. She blamed Mrs. Ingles for making her come out into the wilderness to starve and perish. She threatened to kill her, but Mary managed to talk her out of this notion. By much coaxing, she kept the old woman going. Their corn was entirely gone, and they were again living off whatever fruits or nuts they happened to find. Their shoes had worn out, and their feet were cut and bruised. The fall nights were colder, and they slept little.

Mrs. Ingles felt better when at last they reached the Kanawha River. She recognized the stream without any trouble, and they started up it. They were both so weak that they could hardly walk. Mary had to help the old woman over slippery logs and around rocks where the briars and vines hung thick. They were always hungry.

One day the Dutch woman could stand the hunger pains no longer. She grabbed Mrs. Ingles, saying she was going to kill and eat her. Mary tried to reason with her. She promised the old woman all sorts of presents when they reached Draper's Meadow. But the Dutch woman was beyond such talk. She threw Mrs. Ingles to the ground and raised her tomahawk for the death blow.

5

Home Again

Mary Ingles grabbed the woman's arm and struggled to take the tomahawk away from her. But she was worn out with the long journey and lack of food. The elder woman seemed suddenly to have the strength of madness. They rolled back and forth till at last Mrs. Ingles tore loose from the Dutch woman. She ran and hid in the bushes along the river's edge. The old woman moved off upstream, muttering to herself and tinkling the horse's bell. That night Mrs. Ingles crossed to the opposite bank in the moonlight. She was safe from the old woman, but she was still some distance from home. Weak though she was, she felt she could make it.

Each day thereafter she continued upstream, stumbling, crawling over the rough places, but always moving eastward. Once she came out on the banks of the river and saw on the opposite side her recent companion. The Dutch woman said she was sorry for what had happened. She begged Mary to come and travel with her, and she promised not to harm her. Mrs. Ingles refused. She was too close to Draper's Meadow to take any chances now.

At last she arrived at a cabin that had been overlooked at the time of the raid. Her friends there welcomed her and told her that both her husband and her brother had escaped unhurt from the attack on Draper's Meadow. Mary was overjoyed and asked to see them. She was told that she couldn't, for they were in the Cherokee nation seeking an Indian willing to bargain with the Shawnees for the return of any captives still alive.

They fed Mary then and put her to bed to rest. She made them promise to look for the Dutch woman. The old woman was found and brought in, still clutching the horse's bell. Later she went back to her home in Pennsylvania, and that was the last that was heard of her. If Mrs.

Ingles ever knew her name, it was not recorded. And whenever Mary told of her forty days of hard traveling in the wilderness, her companion was always referred to in the story as "the old Dutch woman."

Thus, by strength and courage and many sorrows and hardships endured, Mary Ingles won her honors and "firsts." Historians say she was the first white woman to see and make salt in the Kanawha River Valley and to visit Kentucky and to make salt there, too, and the first white woman to view the curiosities of Big Bone Lick.

When her husband and brother returned from the Cherokees, there was much to tell each other. The most difficult part for Mary to recount was that she had kissed her daughter good-by and left her among the savages with no hope of seeing her alive ever again. However, there was a possibility that both sons and her sister-in-law might be ransomed from the Indians, and this proved cheerful news to both William Ingles and John Draper.

From that moment William Ingles questioned every person returning from the Shawnee country about his boys. He asked traders for information, but he found out nothing. The French and Indian War was in full swing, and the Indians were on the move constantly. And more and more whites were captured and taken north of the Ohio River. It was almost as much as a man and wife could do in the Great Valley to defend their house and fields and try to farm in between the Indian raids. But they could hope, too, and this Mary and William did.

When peace came, Mrs. John Draper was found by her

husband and ransomed from the Shawnee chieftain. She told, upon her arrival, that George Ingles had died not long after being separated from his mother. Of Thomas, she knew nothing.

Thirteen years were to pass before Thomas Ingles was finally located. Ransom was given, and the boy was brought back to the Great Valley of Virginia. He could speak no English, he dressed as an Indian, and he carried with him at all times his Indian bow and arrows. Mary Ingles persuaded him to wear white men's clothes, but Thomas would not part with his weapons. Often, when he could not stand life at Draper's Meadow, he would take his bow and arrows and go off alone into the woods for days. But each time he returned. He finally married a white girl and went to live in the wilderness. No sooner did he get his wife and children comfortably fixed than he would be seized with restlessness and moved to another spot. There his wild, roving nature would seize him again, and he would go somewhere else. Thus his life continued till his death.

By the close of the French and Indian War, William Ingles had moved to where the Indian War Path crossed New River and had gone into the business of ferryman and tavern keeper. It was a lucrative move, for with the colonies at peace, more and more settlers were traveling west. The easiest route was to follow the War Path down the Great Valley, go beyond the last cabin a few miles, and there make your own clearing. Mary's and William's days as pioneers on the frontier—that outer edge where civilization and wilderness met—were now over. It was time for others to take the place of these two on this line of hazard.

And those who did push on went with the knowledge gained by settlers like the Ingleses. The Great Valley turned out to be a training ground for frontiersmen during the French and Indian War. At its sudden, bloody beginning, many had fled from the valley to safety. But in time they returned and faced up to the dangers and responsibilities of holding a home in the wilderness. In the struggle, they learned many useful things.

Some learned how to farm with one hand and hold a rifle, cocked and ready to shoot, with the other. A few learned to fight in the woods "Indian fashion" from tree to tree. Most learned to endure the cramped quarters of a fort or a blockhouse and wait out the red raiders' siege. All learned that nothing could get in the way of the business of living. Daily tasks had to be done, no matter how often the war whoops sounded or how many fell from blows of the tomahawk.

In time, many leaders in the valley realized that there was no longer any need to stay at home always fearful of raiders. Skirmishing could take place in Indian country; the red men's towns and crops could be destroyed as their own had so often been. From returning captives, such as Mrs. Ingles, a great amount of information was gained about Indian camping sites, salt springs, and trails. Now the initiative could be taken, and this gave the pioneers more confidence. Never again would they flee from the Indians.

There was still much to learn about wilderness living, about plants and trees and the ways of animals. In time, all these things would be mastered. But for now a beginning had been made in the Great Valley, a start toward freedom and one nation from sea to sea.

Mary Ingles outlived her husband and died at the age of eighty-four. After her return from the Shawnees, she and William had four more children, three daughters and one son. It is said that she often recounted to both her children and grandchildren the days when she was taken westward beyond the mountains against her wishes and how there, among savages, she found courage and renewed hope and a will to live.

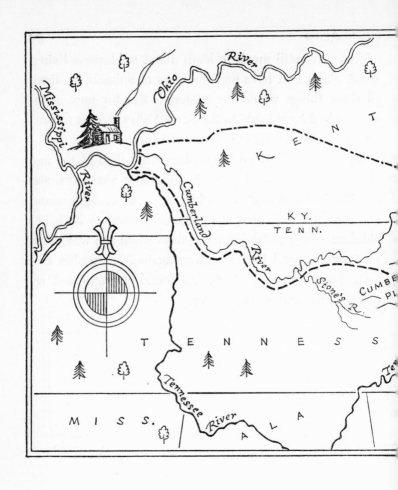

~ *Part Four* ~

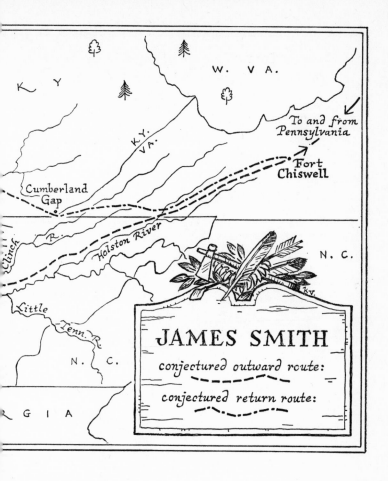

James Smith, explorer, and his knowledge and self-confidence in the uncharted wilds of America in 1766 and '67.

1

Barefoot Men with Their Shoes On

The five travelers turned from the trail and made their way along the bank of the river, stopping finally beneath a cliff. Jamie, a mulatto slave about eighteen years of age, left them to gather wood for a fire. The four white men also began their routine tasks. Joshua Horton and Uriah Stone went off up the stream to hunt with their rifles. William Baker took the blankets, sleeping skins, and other truck from the horses' backs and piled all of it under the rocky ledge. Then he led the animals toward the river and hobbled them where they could graze on the yellow leaves of the cane.

James Smith stood for a moment gazing upward. The wind had risen and was roaring through the valley, lashing the bare branches furiously. Dark gray clouds scudded over and quickly vanished behind the jagged top of the bluff. The cold was sharp. By morning there would be ice at the river's edge. James Smith shrugged. A traveler could hardly expect any other kind of weather in the Appalachian Mountains in December, and it did not matter anyway.

Picking up his tomahawk, Smith made his way over the rocks to a thicket, where he began to chop down tulip-poplar saplings. As he trimmed the fallen trees, he sang a hymn in a loud clear voice, his breath rising like smoke around him in the cold air. Then he dragged the slender poles to the fire Jamie had kindled with flint and steel. He quickly constructed a half-face shelter with sloping roof, pitched so that the open side was toward the fire and the bluff. For the top covering he cut down an elm, slit the whole length of the trunk with his tomahawk, and then pried off long strips of the bark. These he laid over the roof poles as he would shingles.

Snow began to fall, lightly at first, then harder. It covered the twisted pines scraggling from the cracks in the bluff's face and swirled down underneath them into the campfire. Smith surveyed the finished shelter with a critical eye. Let the snow come. It would keep them dry and warm. By comparison with what he had had for protection while an Indian captive, this was a mansion house. More than once he had waited out a cold, icy spell of weather huddled with the red men under an overturned bark canoe, with a few bundles around them serving as the shelter's walls.

Baker had warmed the long-handled axes by the fire to lessen the danger of their breaking in the cold. Now he and Smith walked out into the woods to fell some dead pines. These were dragged up close to the camp. Jamie filled a pot with water and set it over the fire. To one side he left the long-handled frying pan standing on its legs, ready for use.

Smith hunted under the bluff till he found a hard-grained rock that suited him. This he used to sharpen his hunting knife. When the two hunters returned with a deer, Smith was waiting. He slashed one haunch into thick slices to roast around the fire's edge. Strips and collops of the meat he flung into the boiling water. Jamie dressed the two turkeys that had also been brought back. One bird went in the pot with the venison, for these men weren't particular eaters and cared not what kinds of meat were simmering down to a thick stew. Smith cracked the leg bones of the deer and raked the marrow into the pot to add flavor.

Uriah Stone fried a part of the meat in the spider with turkey fat. Baker dipped out some stew with the ladle in which he melted lead for his rifle bullets. When it cooled, he drank it, sopping up the last of it with white meat from the turkey's breast in place of bread. They had brought no corn meal with them to make ash cake. They finished up the meal with hickory and beech nuts collected along the trail that day.

Smith built up the fire, then sat with his back against a log. Flakes of snow, caught in his hair and beard, glimmered in the firelight. Night was almost on them. Nearby a wolf howled, and the horses stamped restlessly at the cry. Soon the animals would have to be picketed close to the bluff. For the moment Smith was too full of good meat and too relaxed to move. He looked around at his companions. They were good travelers and, like himself, knew how to get along in the woods, winter or summer. That was one good thing about men living along the frontier —they were very expert woodsmen. They were like Indians in that respect. He remembered how, years ago, when he had returned from captivity, his people had been surprised to see him acting so much like the red men, both in gait and gesture. He knew the whites had a lot to learn from the Indians about living in the forests.

As soon as he had heard that the lands west of the Appalachians, which lay between the Ohio and Tennessee Rivers, were to be purchased from the northern Indians, he had wanted to "take a tour westward, and explore that country."

He had set out in June, 1766, from his home in Pennsylvania. He had gone down the Valley of Virginia to Fort Chiswell. In that region he had found out about the trails through the mountains. He had also picked out three companions who were as anxious as he was to look over the land on the Western Waters. Now here they were, enjoying themselves and living off the land.

Uriah Stone told that that afternoon he had found some buffalo tracks up the river a short distance. Tomorrow he would return and try to shoot one of the beasts.

Smith said it probably wasn't a buffalo print but that of a Catawba Indian he had seen. Stone answered that he wasn't that stupid. He knew "a B from a buffalo's foot" and these were definitely buffalo hoof marks.

Smith laughed. He explained what he meant. Years ago when he had still been captive among the northern Indians, he was out hunting with a chief named Mohawk Solomon. Smith had found what looked like buffalo tracks. But Mohawk Solomon had told him, "Hush, you know nothing, may be buffaloe tracks, may be Catawba."

Then Solomon had explained about the time the Ca-tawba Indians had come north from their home in Caro-lina. The Catawbas had lain in ambush near the Iroquois hunting camp. To lure the enemy hunters from their camp, several Catawbas had tied buffalo hoofs to their feet and during the night had walked through the camp to make false tracks. The Iroquois saw the tracks the following morning and followed them, thinking they were buffalo. They were fired upon and several were killed.

The Iroquois who escaped aroused the rest of their camp, and all set out in pursuit of the Catawbas. The Carolina Indians had brought with them rattlesnake poison corked up in a short piece of cane stalk. The sharpened ends of cane were dipped in this poison, and then the canes were hidden in the grass among the Catawbas' tracks in such a position that they might stick into the legs of the pursuing Iroquois.

Mohawk Solomon said soon many of the Iroquois were limping from "being artificially snakebit." Finally the Iroquois stopped the chase and headed back toward their camp. Then the Catawbas fell on all those who were lame and killed and scalped them.

Smith looked around the fire at his companions and grinned. He would never forget what Mohawk Solomon had said when he finished telling the story. He had turned to Smith and said, "You don't know, Catawba velly bad Indian, Catawba all one Devil Catawba."

Smith said that was the reason these might not be buffalo tracks but Catawba Indians. Stone was much amused at the story and promised to be careful the following day when he hunted. However, he, as well as the others, knew the Catawbas were no longer to be feared. Smallpox had almost wiped out the once great tribe, and those who survived were living peacefully on a reservation in South Carolina.

The men began to tell of the days when they had fought the Indians. As they talked, they kept busy. Smith took a piece of deerskin and his awl and used these to patch a hole in the side of his moccasin. Stone and Horton dried their footwear near the fire, stuffing moss and leaves inside to preserve the shape. Later they would rub turkey fat into the moccasins. They might be a "decent way of going barefooted," but they were essential to woodsmen. They were light and comfortable to wear, soundless in the woods and easily made. But the men had to dry their moccasins as often as possible. Constant wearing of wet ones gave their feet a burning sensation, an affliction called "scald foot."

There was lead to melt and pour into the bullet molds, rifles to clean, and many other tasks to perform before going to bed. At last, however, everything was done, and the men went to sleep under the half-faced shelter, their feet toward the fire.

The following morning when they arose, there was over a foot of snow on the ground. Snow didn't bother them, but the hard crust on top of the snow did. Now they would not be able to sneak up on any game, for each step would break through the crust and make a noise. Smith suggested that their best chance was to hunt bear holes. So after breakfast they set out in pairs.

Stone and Horton went in one direction with their long-handled axes in case they had to cut down a hollow tree to get to the bear. Smith did not care to tote an ax. He had a piece of dry fungus inside of which he placed a glowing wood coal. The fungus would smolder but not flame up. He put this in a piece of hollow deer antler and set off with Baker.

By noon they had found a huge tree from which the bark had been scratched by bear claws. About forty feet overhead was a hole. Smith collected some rotten wood and tied it in bundles with vines. Then he climbed up the trunk to the hole. Taking out his smoldering fungus, he set the rotten wood on fire. When it was smoking mightily, he dropped first one bundle of it, then the other, down the hole. Then he scrambled to the ground.

He and Baker waited with their rifles ready. Smoke poured out of the hole. Suddenly they heard a muffled growl, then a thumping and scratching. Now a bear appeared in the opening, looking sleepily around. As it edged out to get away from the smoke, Smith shot it. They dragged it back to camp over the snow.

Jamie had stayed behind to keep the fire going and to tend to the horses. The pot with the left-over venison-turkey stew stood at the edge of the fire. Into this Smith tossed pieces of bear meat, added water and salt, and set it to boiling again.

Then he took the bear's liver out "and wrapped some of

the caul fat round and put it on a wooden spit." This he
stuck in the ground by the fire to roast slowly. Later,
when the other hunters returned, this liver was used as
sauce for the roasted bear's flesh, and all said it was
"delicate fare."

Thus, the explorers passed the winter months hunting
and eating and talking. Smith kept a journal in which he
recorded their adventures or sometimes his judgment of
the land through which they passed. When he found a
stand of beech he wrote that these "spots may be called
third rate land," though if spicewood grew there too, it
might be second rate. The best land, first and second rate,
had ash, walnut, sugar tree, honey locust, red haw, and
cherry trees on it, though not every one judging land by
this method used the very same trees or reached the same
conclusions. Generally, most people agreed that black and
post oak always denoted very poor soil.

Sometimes the men sang hymns or read psalms, for
Smith was greatly interested in religion. During his captivity he had read a book of sermons and a Bible taken
from settlers killed by his Indian hosts. Often they moved
their camping place from the banks of one stream over a
ridge and down a valley to that of another, and each time
it was farther and farther to the west, toward the vacant
inland part of the continent.

2

A Desperate Case

It is not known which route these men took, either going or returning. There were two possible existing Indian trails leading westward. There was one route through Cumberland Gap. Doctor Thomas Walker had discovered this gap in 1750, and it had been used ever since by hunters. Fort Chiswell, where Smith picked up his companions, was in later years the starting point for Long Hunters who used Cumberland Gap to reach the game-filled savannas of Kentucky as well as those of Tennessee.

There was a more southern route across the Cumberland Plateau, an Indian trail that came to be known as Avery's Trace and, after that, as Walton's Road. Travelers using this way much later in the century complained of the "barren and broken" country and of the route's roughness, for it was "full of rock slabs which, often elevated, lie straight across the road." Perhaps this is the reason Smith noted that "it was difficult to take a horse through the mountains."

Or it could have been that Smith's party did not use an Indian trail at all and so had great difficulty passing through the mountain. Usually, though, adventurers would follow a trace, leaving it to explore or to hunt but coming back to it to push toward their destination.

Whichever route these men took, they must surely have gone along indulging themselves in the usual explorer custom of labeling the springs, the mountains, and the rivers with their own names. It was the privilege of those who first spied out the land. And sometimes the names stuck.

The mountains behind them now, the group reached a south branch of the Cumberland River, which they called Stone's River. "We first gave it this name in our journal in May, 1767, after one of my fellow travellers, Mr. Uriah Stone." Today, the river is still called by that name.

This is one of the few definite points located by Smith in the short account of his journey. It is enough to show that he had found that large body of rich land of which he had heard from conversing with the Indians in their own tongue. This region along the Cumberland River in middle Tennessee was one of the loveliest and most bountiful found so far by the white colonists in eastern America. It was an earthly paradise, a Garden of Eden, rivaling those lands of plenty found in medieval travelers' tales.

Here was an open country of grassy savannas, with scattered parklike groves in which the trees were widely spaced. Along the streams, the low meadows were a tangle of wild sweet clover, and cane grew thirty or forty feet high in brakes that stretched for miles. There was a great variety of trees on the low hills, which were not "choaked up with underbrush," so that it was easy to go through on horseback or on foot. In glades, strawberries "covered the ground as with a red cloth."

No Indians lived here, but both northern and southern tribes considered it their hunting ground. And there was plenty of game to hunt: herds of elk feeding on fern in the woodlands; deer and bear and turkey picking at the mast of acorns and chestnuts and beechnuts falling to the ground in a steady rain through the frosty autumns; swans and geese and ducks of all kinds on the streams. And best of all there were big shaggy creatures each with "a Bunch on its Back like a Camel."

The buffalo herds were never as great as those of the western plains, but still the numbers were impressive around the licks where they gathered to wallow and roll in the miry puddles and to drink the salt and sulphur waters. One Long Hunter told of a spring he discovered in this area where there was "such a crowd of buffellows in the Lick and around it" that he was afraid to get off his horse for fear of being trampled into the mud as were two deer he had killed.

The buffalo had only in recent time spread out from their homeland on the plains and begun to disperse over the eastern part of North America. A peninsula of prairie-like land extended down from Illinois across Kentucky and into middle Tennessee, and this was where the largest number of the animals were found east of the Mississippi River.

Smith said he and his party "explored the Cumberland and Tennessee Rivers, from Stone's River down to the Ohio." They met no white men nor any Indians. At the mouth of the Tennessee River the men from the Valley of

Virginia wanted to go on to see the Illinois country, for they had heard much about the rich grassy plains there.

Smith was unwilling to go with them. His wife would think he had been killed by Indians if he stayed away any longer. He would go back home. Mr. Horton lent him the mulatto boy, Jamie, and Smith gave them his horse. They gave Smith most of the ammunition, "half a pound of powder, and lead equivalent," as they could swap his horse for ammunition with the traders or at the forts in the French-dominated Illinois country. Smith was returning through an unsettled country and would need all the ammunition the others could spare.

Eight days after they split up, Smith and Jamie were making their way along a path that led through cane. The jointed stalks grew up around them like a forest. A breeze rattled the long dried leaves. The tasseled tops swayed high in the air. Smith picked his way carefully. When cane broke near the ground, a stub was left sticking up. This was razor-sharp and dangerous. Indians who lacked flint often made a temporary knife from a piece of cane, using the glasslike outer layer for the cutting edge.

In spite of Smith's care, he stepped on a cane stob. It went through his moccasin and into his flesh. He jerked his foot away and inspected the wound. It bled little, so he tied his shoe back on and continued. By the time they left the cane and moved in among the trees, Smith was limping. A piece of the stob had broken off in his foot. Still he was unwilling to stop and went on following the trail. His leg began to swell and hurt terribly every time he put his weight on it. At last he was forced to halt.

What could he do? There was no doctor to remove the snag from his foot. He had no horse to carry him, and he could walk no further. His case appeared desperate.

3

The Cure of the Cane-Stob Stab

James Smith sat on the ground, his back against a tree, his legs stretched out before him. The trail wound away from him, off through the trees. Where the woods was open, the August sunlight sent heat waves dancing along the path. Behind him a woodpecker drummed on a dead tree, called once, and flew away. Mosquitoes buzzed about him, and a midge flew into his ear. He shook his head in irritation. He was tired, almost too tired to decide what to do.

Jamie waited patiently beside him, squatting on his heels. He had on only a breechclout made by Smith for him some time ago. His moccasins were full of holes.

Smith could direct Jamie in the making of an Indian travois from poles and vines. He could lie on it and let the mulatto boy drag him to the nearest settlement. But it would be a rough ride, bumping over rocks and roots. It might be too much for Jamie's strength. And it would take too long.

Smith looked down at his swollen foot and leg. The skin was stretched tight, and as high as his knee, it was blotched and red. Infection would kill him before he ever arrived anywhere near the settlements on a travois.

The only other choice left him was to take the piece of cane from his foot. He grimaced. It would be a nasty job, probing for the splinter, but he didn't want Jamie doing it. He would do it himself. But not here, not here on the trail where they would be helpless to any passing Indians.

He told Jamie what his plans were. The colored boy nodded and helped him to stand. Placing an arm around Jamie's shoulder, Smith hopped away from the trace and back among the trees a good distance. At each jump pain went shooting up his leg in hot, quick jabs.

At last they found a suitable place. Jamie lowered the white man to the ground. Sweat poured down Smith's face and neck. He was dizzy with pain. He wiped the sweat from his eyes and took from the blanket roll his "surgical instruments." There was a bullet mold, a knife with a well-honed blade, and a small awl he used to patch his moccasins. These were certainly not much, but he had no choice. They would have to do. He would get to work and take his chance.

Gritting his teeth hard, he stuck the awl into his foot and began to feel around for the piece of cane. A watery, yellowish liquid oozed from the hole. He struck a bone and grunted. Where was that piece of cane? The pain was almost unbearable.

He rested a moment, looking up at Jamie. The boy

grinned feebly, waiting for any directions Smith would give him. He was a willing worker and always did as he was told. The two had gotten along fine together so far.

Smith took the awl once again and felt this way and that with the pointed end. And at last he found the splinter. Snatching up his knife, he cut away the flesh from around the cane so that one end of it was left sticking up.

He handed the bullet mold to Jamie and told him to use it as he would pliers. The boy took the two handles, and opening it, he seized the piece of cane with the two halves of the mold, as with the jaws of pliers. He gave a jerk and out came the long, jagged cane splinter. He held it up for the white man to see.

"It seemed a shocking thing to be in any person's foot," Smith said, and he was very relieved to have it out.

Smith lay back on the ground. His foot was still in bad shape, and he must do something further to help the wound to heal. He had nothing of use in his blanket pack. Indian medicine was all around him in the woods, but what would be the best to use?

He decided that perhaps basswood or linden tree bark would be just the thing. Its inner bark had long, tough fibers, which, with much work, could be made into rope, but when this bark was soaked in water, it became sticky as glue. The Indians had long used it to heal wounds such as his.

He sent Jamie off for some bark from the "lynn tree," as he called it. When the boy brought it, Smith instructed him to pound it into fine pieces with Smith's tomahawk. These pieces were boiled in the small brass pot. Then Smith bathed his foot and leg in the juice, cooking what was left till it was a sticky jelly. He had no rags to bind his wound. But he spread the linden jelly on strips of green moss, which he had pulled from a log. He wrapped these around his foot and tied them in place with elm bark.

In a few days he was much better; his leg was no longer inflamed and swollen. Still he could not walk on it. Jamie had made them a half-face shelter, covering it with cane tops "like a fodder-house." But there was no food. So the two went back to the path, Jamie with the rifle and Smith hopping on one leg from tree to tree. They hid in the bushes and waited beside the trail.

Soon, along came a single file of buffalo, their hard hoofs kicking up a cloud of dust. They stopped to crop the grass where the path was wide, the little new calves staying close to their mothers' sides. An old bull dropped down in the dust of the path. He rubbed his head hard, gouging up the earth with his horn. Then he rolled over on his great hump to his other side and rubbed around till he was covered with dust.

Smith waited patiently for one of the beasts to graze closer. He did not have much ammunition, and he wanted to make sure he killed with the first shot, for it might be the only one he had. Buffalo were easily frightened.

The bull got to its feet and shook. Dust flew from its hairy coat. One of the cows gave a startled snort and trotted away from the rest. Down the path, toward where Smith and Jamie lay, the cow came. Smith took careful aim with his long rifle and fired. The cow fell. The rest of the buffalo galloped away with their tails raised.

Jamie and Smith wouldn't go hungry now, for a buffalo furnished not only a great amount of meat but a variety also. The tongue was tender and tasty when roasted. The hump was greasy but such delicious eating that many hunters preferred it to the tongue. These two cuts were the best part of the buffalo, but haunches broiled by the fire were good, as were the fleece ribs. Any time this kind of fare became tiresome, one of the marrowbones could be cracked open and the marrow fat, or "hunter's butter," could be used to spread on and flavor the meat.

Wisely, they "jirked" what meat they could not eat right away. A scaffold was built, and slices of buffalo were roasted on this till the strips were dried thoroughly. This jerk was tough to chew, but it would keep for a long time without spoiling. Stewed with tallow, it was not only delicious but also very sustaining in the woods.

James Smith lay in his hut, filled with buffalo meat and later, when that gave out, elk, and read two books he had with him. One was a Psalm Book, the other Watts upon prayer. When he was tired of those, he composed verses to sing. What kind of life was this for a man as active as this explorer? It must have been a satisfying one if one of the verses he made up can be taken for fact.

> "This doleful circumstance cannot
> My happiness prevent,
> While peace of conscience I enjoy
> Great comfort and content."

4

This New American

The summer passed into the fall, and at last Smith was well enough to travel. By October, he and Jamie were "in Carolina." Where this was and what route they used to come there, Smith does not say. He had explored to the west for eleven months, and when he arrived in Carolina with Jamie, they were dressed in what they had made while in the wilderness. To buckskin outfits of breech-clout, leggings, and moccasins, Smith had added a beaver hat and Jamie a raccoon cap and a bear skin, which he wore belted around him. Wherever they went, they alarmed the dogs, and even the people were amazed and a little scared at their appearance.

There was something almost magical, and certainly there was something very wonderful, in the way James Smith wandered out into the unknown wilderness during the coldest months of the year with a meager amount of equipment and yet provided himself with adequate food, shelter, and clothing and, in time of sickness, with medicine. How could he manage such a feat?

He could do it because he was no longer an English colonist but an "American, this new man." He went out of a love and longing for freedom and adventure that made him certain that whatever trials and tribulations he endured would be worthwhile. He went armed with a rifle, a new and different and better weapon than the awkward musket brought from Europe. He carried an ax, not the straight-handled, wobbly old tool that Englishmen had used since Roman times, but a new whip-handled, agile ax that was marvelously adapted to the tasks of the New World—cutting the great trees, clearing trails, building log cabins and bridges, shaping trenchers and benches.

And most important, he took with him the long lore gained from the generations of families who, in adapting themselves to forest living, had conquered the wilderness and learned the knack of survival. He knew how to fight, how to hunt, how to travel light and fast in the forests. He knew which plants were good for food and which for medicines and which were poisonous. Meals, remedies, shelter, clothing, all were available in the woods, and Smith knew how to get them.

He went into the forests confident that here he was master, that his knowledge and skills and energy could overcome any obstacle. He set his face toward the West without regret.

When James Smith got back to civilization, he returned to Fort Chiswell and left Jamie at Mr. Horton's Negro quarters, as he had promised. Then he journeyed on to his wife and children in Pennsylvania, his exploring days finished. He did not settle on the Western Waters till some twenty years later when he moved to Kentucky.

But he must never have forgotten those pleasant days, when, assured and unafraid, he tramped the hills and far-off valleys of a new country—the "American, this new man."

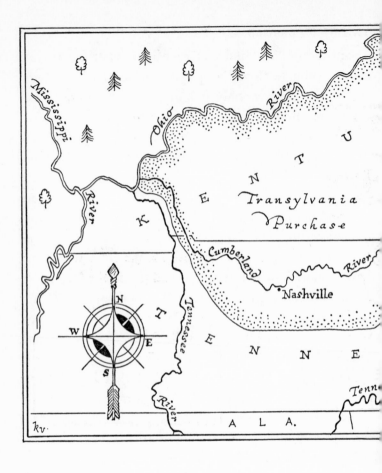

~ *Part Five* ~

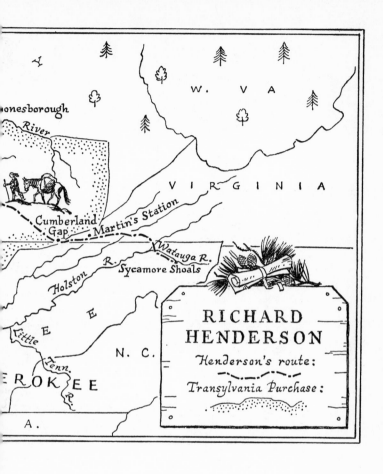

Richard Henderson, colonizer, and his dream of an empire in the Dark and Bloody Land in 1775.

1

"What a Buzzel!"

Caintuck! Kentuck! However it was spelled or pronounced, the mere mention of it made a man's heart beat faster. Kentucky! There was a tingling magic in the name that stirred rich and poor alike, so that all burned with a great desire to see that far-off, fabulous land beyond the mountains.

For some time, those who had been there and returned spread the news of its wonders throughout the back country of the colonies. They said:

"In Kaintuck there's miles and miles of cane brakes along the river bottoms. Why, that's how come it's called Canetuck, and the cane grows so thick the rivers can't force their way through the stalks, but have to go round. And the ground's so rich a man dastn't go barefoot for fear his toes will take root. There's salt licks a-plenty and there's a great heap of game too, all rolling fat and weary for the rifle shot. The bones of some of the varmints in Kentuck are so big, a body can set down on a piece of backbone and make tent poles out of the ribs. And trees, gracious, they grow high enough to shut out the sunlight and wide enough to fill a whole field. And there ain't a single Injun what lives in Kentuck 'cause they're scared of all the human blood that's been spilled there—ain't they the foolish ones?"

It must have been hard for the stay-at-homes to tell the truth from the dreams. The land *was* rich, a luscious, rolling meadowland. The cane did stretch for miles and miles along the winding rivers, crowding out all other plant life. There *was* a salt lick where the great bones of extinct animals lay, just as gigantic as they were described to be. There was a great amount of game—bear, elk, buffalo, turkeys, and all kinds of waterfowl. It is doubtful, even in Kentuck where strange things turned out to be real, that the game was begging to be shot or that the ducks were so numerous that a hunter didn't have to shoot them, but just waited till enough were killed by being pushed into the current and swept over the rocky falls. And who can judge whether the pioneer preacher had reliable information or not when he told his congregation in a sermon, "O my dear honeys, heaven is a Kentucky of a place." Too many stories were being told, and the truth about Kentucky seemed the stuff of legends.

And so there were many men who discounted all the stories of Caintuck. They had heard this kind of talk before about other places of milk and honey. They were not going to be misled once again by such land fever. Perhaps it was just such a doubter who said, "What a Buzzel is amongst People about Kentuck! To hear people speak of it one would think it was a new found Paradise."

This "Buzzel" grew even louder after the Shawnee Indians were defeated by the backwoodsmen at the Battle of Point Pleasant, which took place at the mouth of the Kanawha River. Then the Ohio River became the definite southern boundary of the tribe's land. Never again was a Shawnee supposed to cross that river into Kentucky to hunt or even to make salt. That was the second tribe to relinquish their hunting rights there, the Iroquois being the first. So talk of the lush and green meadowlands increased, for, it seemed, the time had surely come to settle in Kentucky.

However, the "Buzzel" reached its greatest fervor when the news was spread throughout the back country of Virginia and North Carolina that Kentuck was being bought by one man. The restless, land-hungry frontiersmen were disappointed that someone had beat them to that rich country. But there was disbelief, too. Buy Kentuck! A boundary, a line could be run around such a mythical land, and it could be bought by one as some household item was bought? Such a possibility staggered the minds of the backwoods settlers. It was difficult to believe.

But it was true. A great sale was taking place at Sycamore Shoals on the Watauga River. All who could get there by shanks' mare or on solid horse flesh came to see the man who was buying Kentucky and to see the Indians who were selling the land. They came, too, to stand and stare at the log cabin in which was kept the merchandise that was to be traded for Kentucky.

Men, women, and children, whole families of them, stood before the cabin with awe and wonder. In one single room was enough to buy Canetuck. Surely it would take more than that. Perhaps there was gold in there, too. Very few of them got a look inside that log house, and so speculation as to what goods were there was unrestrained.

Some feared there were cannons and rifles inside and that by next week the Cherokees would be on the warpath, trying to drive them from their clearings in the forests. Others said it was only baubles and pretties for the Indian women and children. Rumor said the goods were worth ten thousand pounds sterling. But some doubted it was so much, and the value was sworn to be only eight, then six, thousand.

Money was seldom seen in the backwoods, and it was much easier to comprehend the price to be paid for Kentucky in terms of wagonloads. One said what was in that cabin amounted to "only ten waggons loaded with cheap goods such as coarse woolens, trinkets and spiritous liquors." This, in time, was denied, as many claimed to have seen only six wagons creak past their houses to this place. And so the talk continued and none knew, for how could a man place a price on the rich lands of Kentuck?

When the curious tired of this guessing game, they could drift over to the pits of hot coals where whole bears, deer, hogs, and beeves were roasting. They could sniff the baking ashcakes and long for some of this food. But it was not for them. It was to feed the Indian chieftains and their families. Since the first of the year, the red men had been arriving at Sycamore Shoals in anticipation of the food and the gifts they would receive from this sale. It was probably the greatest gathering of Cherokee chieftains in that nation's history, and the frontiersmen were there to see them.

And when the onlookers were tired of the sights of the treaty ground, they could always gather together and discuss the man who was buying Kentucky. The Colonial Governor of Virginia had issued a proclamation against this man, calling him and his associates "disorderly persons." The Governor of North Carolina said they were "an infamous Company of Land Pyrates."

Who was this man who had upset so many people, who had been smart enough to organize a company and buy Kentucky? He had been a lawyer. He had been a judge, too, in the North Carolina courts. He was neither now, but that hardly mattered, for this man was about to own more land than anybody else in America. And he wanted settlers and was willing to sell tracts of land to them. Daniel Boone was already making a road through the mountains so that any who came to Kentuck would have no trouble traveling there. And talk was that Kentucky was soon to be called Transylvania and was to be the fourteenth British colony on this continent.

The frontiersmen at the gathering at Sycamore Shoals watched this man with respect, and they spoke his name often. It was Richard Henderson, Colonel Richard Henderson.

2

Melted Snowballs

In the cabin Richard Henderson stood and picked up his great coat. It was time for him to go to the treaty grounds and begin the second day of talks. Would today, March 15, 1775, be the day he bought the land and became the owner of an empire? There was not a chief against the sale of the title to the Cherokee hunting lands beyond the Appalachians—twenty million acres of the best land in America. Daniel Boone and other hunters had assured Henderson it was the finest land imaginable.

Colonel Henderson and his associates in the Transylvania Company were going to buy it all for a cabinful of goods. The merchandise was right here in this very room with him. Guns were stacked in one corner, with barrels of black powder and bars of lead beside them. There were bolts of red calico and green durance, piles of "Dutch blankets," and scores of bundles of fancy shirts. Lining one wall were wallets of salt and corn flour and "other necessaty's to a great amount." Beyond those were boxes of wristbands and metal gorgets and brooches, then rolls of colored ribbons and all kinds of other baubles.

It was an excellent assortment of goods, and it certainly ought to have been. Attakullakulla and another Cherokee brave, as well as an Indian woman, had inspected and approved the lot last fall. It had taken six wagons to haul all of it to this cabin beside the Watauga River.

Henderson put on his great coat, clapped his hat on his head, and moved toward the cabin door. He knew of nothing to prevent them from buying this land, and unless the chiefs felt the urge to talk at great length, the actual papers might be signed today. He hoped so. But he wanted it all to take place in a legal fashion. He believed in law and order. And in spite of what the colonial governors and officials said about him, he felt that he was within his rights as a private citizen in dealing with the Cherokee nation.

He lifted the door latch and stepped outside. The good smell of cooking meat was in the air, and the shouts from the treaty grounds were loud enough to drown out the roar of the shoals beyond the cabin. There were close to twelve hundred Indians here. It was costing a lot to feed them, but it would be worth the price, for food and drink kept Indians in a happy frame of mind. When all the papers were signed, he would give them rum—but not till everything was over and finished. He didn't want anyone to accuse him of getting the Cherokees drunk and then stealing their land. He wanted to purchase the land only in fair and open treaty.

Walking under the sycamore trees, the colonel made his way toward where the chiefs and the Transylvania members awaited him. To one side, two white men were bargaining for an Indian's horse. The animal was handsome and spirited, of the kind called "Chickasaw breed."

It was said they could run all day, being "long-winded, like wolves." He passed by Indian children playing games and groups of women "as fair and blooming as European women."

He called out to acquaintances in the crowd, John Sevier, the Robertson brothers, Isaac Shelby, and a couple of Indian traders. There were several men here from Virginia. They had traveled quite a way to see the goings-on. He smiled. The back country was certainly stirred up over the purchase of this land.

He scanned the sky. There was a scattering of clouds over toward the mountains, but it should be clear the whole day, he judged. The wind had a chill in it, and he was glad he had worn his great coat. Still, for March, this was fine weather. Fine for road builders, too. How far could Boone and his axmen have gone? Many had told him Boone shouldn't have been sent off five days ago before the papers even were signed. But Henderson wanted that road ready. The moment this business was done, he was heading for Kentuck to see what he had bought.

He jostled his way through the ring of onlookers and into the cleared center of the gathering. Making sure his own interpreter, the Indian trader Thomas Price, was present, Henderson nodded to Joseph Vann to begin. Vann was the official translator for Britain's southern Indian Department, which did not approve of this meeting, and was here contrary to his duty. But he claimed he needed the extra money, and he was very familiar with this kind of meeting, so Henderson had hired him.

The colonel dropped down beside Nathaniel Hart and John Luttrell, two members of the Transylvania Company. He asked Price about the chances on winding this business up today, and the old trader pointed out that all the chiefs seemed ready to sign. Henderson nodded, reassured, and turned his attention to the Indians seated opposite him.

From among the red men rose one who was "of remarkable small stature, slender and of a delicate frame." His ears were cut and banded with silver, and these hoops hung down to his shoulders. It was Attakullakulla. He was called by the colonists the Little Carpenter because he was skillful at bringing into agreement the differences between white and red men, much as a carpenter "could bring every notch and joint to fit in wood."

Attakullakulla spoke and stopped. Vann translated what he said for the assembly, sentence by sentence. The Indian chieftain told how, as a youth, he had journeyed to England with six other Cherokees and Eleazer Wiggan. They were the first Cherokees to go there. And now all of that group were dead except him. He had liked the great king across the water and would be happy to visit England again. But he had no time for such pleasures because his people kept him busy. He wanted Henderson to know that the Cherokees had a rightful title to the lands they were selling. He was in favor of the sale because his people never went into those lands to the west to hunt "but that they ran with Blood."

Henderson sighed to himself. He wished the Indians wouldn't talk so much. They were as dull to listen to as the white lawyers in the court where he had once been the judge. His glance strayed to some of the other chiefs seated behind Attakullakulla.

There was Oconostota, the Great Warrior, a large man with smallpox scars on his face. He approved of the sale, Henderson knew, though the chief seldom talked at these treaty meetings. Traders had told the colonel it was because Oconostota was "dull in point of intellect." The chief always said his words were too blunt for such gatherings and that his nephew, Savanooka, the Raven, would speak for him. Savanooka sat straight-backed and proud-looking beside Oconostota. It was said that the Raven won all the athletic contests among the Cherokees. To Henderson, he looked powerful enough to take on the North Carolina militia singlehanded.

On the other side of Savanooka sat the Old Tassel. Then came Abram of Chilhowie, the Hanging Maw, and finally Bloody Fellow. Henderson's eyes went down this line of older chiefs and back. Nothing could be told from the stiff expressions of their faces, but not a one had been against this sale when he talked to them in their villages last fall.

Behind them were many of the younger chiefs. These had not yet distinguished themselves in battle or in diplomacy for the nation, and Henderson knew very few of their names. Price had told him to ignore them, as they would likely not speak, and if they did, they would only echo what the older chieftains said. They would not dare ruin this sale if their elders sanctioned it.

Behind the chiefs were many warriors, some dressed in

white men's clothes—scarlet coats and ruffled shirts and three-cornered hats with lace piping. Others had blankets around their shoulders. Some were in breechclouts, with silver bands around their forearms, mirrors hanging on strings from their necks. Beyond the braves were the women, all decked out in their best calicoes and silks. Their hair was shiny with bear's oil and plaited with colored ribbons. The Cherokees in their bright dress were quite a contrast to the somber backwoods folks' clothing of homespun stained with plant dyes of browns and grays and dull yellows.

Attakullakulla finished his talk and sat down. Another chief rose to speak. The morning passed slowly. At one point the Cherokees tried to sell land that they had once sold to the colony of Virginia and for which they had never been paid. But Henderson refused to consider this offer, saying he would take his cabinful of goods and go back to his home in Hillsborough, North Carolina. He wanted the lands between "the mouth of Kentucky, Ehenoca, or what, by the English, is called Louisa River" and the Cumberland River "including all its waters." He had Joseph Vann fairly and truly translate the boundaries from the treaty papers so that all the Cherokees would understand perfectly what lands they were selling when they signed the papers.

There was a murmur among the Indians when Vann had finished interpreting the boundaries. Several of the older chiefs nodded in agreement. But many of the warrior spectators scowled, and several spoke out angrily.

The colonel turned to his own interpreter and asked if Vann had tricked him in the translating. Price said no. He then explained to Henderson that many of the warriors felt that too much of the hunting land was being sold, that their children would now starve without these lands.

Suddenly one of the young chieftains stood and, drawing his blanket about him, walked haughtily forward to stand facing Henderson. It was Dragging Canoe, the son of Attakullakulla. His town was on Big Island in the Little Tennessee River.

Dragging Canoe began to speak. He told of the former greatness of the Ani-Yunwiya, the Real People—how they had held the lands against ancient enemies, waging battle after battle to make sure their children would always have a place to live, a place to hunt. At the mountain passes and along many of the old trails were piles of stones to commemorate the places where Cherokee heroes died holding back the enemy. These were hallowed spots, as were the "old fields" where towns had once stood and the places where the bones of their fathers and grandfathers rested. Many stories and legends had grown up about the Cherokee rivers where the water cannibals lived and about the Cherokee mountains where the slant-eyed giant walked and where Uktena, the jewel-headed snake, lurked.

Bit by bit these sacred places had been given up to satisfy the greed of the white man for land. And always the white man demanded more. The Cherokees had once hoped the whites would not reach the lands beyond the mountains, but now they had. And now they wanted to buy all of it, all of the best hunting lands of the nation. Soon all of the country that the Cherokees and their fathers had long occupied would be gone. And the Real People would be forced to live like wild animals in the wilderness with no land to call their own.

Whole nations of Indians had already vanished, "melted away like balls of snow in the sun." He did not want that to happen to his people. He would not let it happen. He would not accept such a treaty as Henderson demanded. Let his father, let the other men who were too old to hunt and fight, let *them* accept the treaty.

Dragging Canoe drew himself up, tall and proud. In his eyes there was fury. He finished, "As for me, I have my young warriors about me. We will have our lands. A-wan-inski, I have spoken."

The Canoe turned and left the gathering. There were cries and shouts of agreement from among the onlooking warriors. Many followed the young chief away from the meeting. The old chiefs sat immobile, their faces masking whatever they felt about this sudden turn of events. Attakullakulla looked at the ground. The Raven tried to quiet the Cherokees in the circle around the officials so the treaty talk could continue. But it was useless. Dragging Canoe's speech had stirred them up too much.

Colonel Henderson told Vann to tell the Indians the meeting would go on tomorrow morning. Right now, it was time to eat. Tell the Cherokees to eat heartily; there would be fiddle music for their entertainment.

Then Richard Henderson stood up and silently watched the red men drift off toward the cooking pits. He was disappointed, and he was terribly worried. Young Cherokee chieftains seldom went against the wishes of their fathers. Certainly not in a public meeting such as this one. And Attakullakulla had favored the sale. Would he still be for it after this fiery talk by his son?

Henderson sighed. Was this the end of his colony in Kentuck?

3

To "Flusterate" or Not?

That same night the Indians held their own council. And the Little Carpenter prevailed upon them to accept the offer of Henderson and the Transylvania Company. It may be that he realized the land would soon be settled anyway, if not by these men, then by some other whites. He may have pointed out to his Cherokee companions that other Indian nations claimed the land too and hunted there. Why shouldn't the Ani-Yunwiya, the Real People, have the cabinful of goods instead of some wretched nation like the Chickasaw, who thought the land was really theirs?

Whatever argument Attakullakulla or the other old chiefs used, it worked. On St. Patrick's Day, March 17,

1775, the title to the lands passed from the Cherokees to the nine members of the Transylvania Company, "their heirs and assigns forever." Three representatives of the nation signed the legal document with their marks, Oconostota, Attakullakulla, and Savanooka.

Dragging Canoe still protested the sale, especially when Henderson asked for additional ground, that land through which the path to Kentucky ran, saying he "did not love to walk over their land." He bought this with "some Goods, Guns, Ammunition which they had not yet seen." At this, Dragging Canoe stamped his foot, and pointing to the west, said that there was "a dark cloud over that country" and that Henderson would find its settlement "bloody."

The young chief's exact words may have been phrased differently, for no one took them down at the time. Yet from those who reported later what he said, it would seem that the Canoe first attached the name of the "Dark and Bloody Ground" to Kentucky and to middle Tennessee. And it was to prove an apt one.

Dragging Canoe's protest had been made in a very dramatic fashion, but it was no idle gesture. From this meeting till his death in 1792, the Canoe fought the American settlers. He burned their cabins, scalped their children, and killed men and women in raid after raid along the frontier. He has been pitied for trying to turn back the Americans with his handful of followers and thus pictured as a tragic figure in the history of the Old Southwest. Those who hold this assumption have forgotten that warfare was the ancient and noble way of life for an Indian. The Canoe kept his self-respect as a warrior by choosing to fight for his nation's lands. To him, the white path of peace that his father traveled led only to humiliation.

The Canoe did not lack for followers among the young men when the cabinful of goods was divided among the Cherokees. Many received so little as their share that they were keenly dissatisfied. One brave was heard to complain with bitterness that he had sold land on which he could kill enough deer in a day to buy his portion of the treaty goods—one white shirt. Now the hunting grounds to the west were gone forever.

If a large number of the Cherokees were unhappy as a result of the meeting at Sycamore Shoals, Richard Henderson was certainly not. After years of careful planning and with a great deal of expense, he at last had a vast, unsettled tract of the richest land on the continent. And he was going to sell it "to a large number of honest farmers, artificers, etc.," or to any "Emigrant or Adventurers" who wished to settle there. On the Western Waters he was establishing the colony of Transylvania, the first to be added to the original thirteen.

Others before him had dreamed of a colony in the interior of the continent, but no one had ever come as close to making his efforts a reality as had Henderson. Setting out for Kentucky with two of the company's members, Nathaniel Hart and John Luttrell, it must have seemed to Henderson that the hardest part of the enterprise was completed. Enjoyment of his success and a chance of wealth lay ahead. It would be a pleasant adventure to travel over the road Boone had marked out for him, and he looked forward to a journey filled with "Novelties." His brother, Samuel, and William Cocke were in charge of the wagons and the pack horses. Others were driving the herd of cattle that Henderson took to keep from losing time hunting game for the large number of men. There was nothing to worry about except reaching his property and taking possession of it.

The route the cavalcade followed had been one of a vast network of Indian trails in eastern America long before the white man arrived. Frontiersmen had finally discovered and used it to reach the game-filled savannas of Tennessee and Kentucky on their long hunts a good many years before Daniel Boone traveled over it on his well-known exploration journeys. In time, it was to become the most significant passageway through the Appalachian Mountain barrier for the westward-moving settlers and to be called "Boone's Path," "The Wilderness Road," "the Road to Caintuck," and many other names. Although Boone and his thirty axmen had cut away the brush along the sides and cleared the path of fallen trees, there was little they could do about the rocky ground where the trail climbed the mountains and followed the streams. It was too rough for the wagons, and they fell behind at the start.

Henderson and the others on horseback went on to wait for the vehicles at Martin's Station in Powell Valley. Joseph Martin had attempted a settlement there in 1769, but the Indians had driven him away. Now with the colonel's support he was trying once again. He and his men had built six cabins and connected them with a stockade of logs. At one corner of the enclosure was a good spring. It was a formidable fort and a safe place to rest before attempting the climb through Cumberland Gap and the remaining half of the rough road through the wilderness.

Henderson spent several days at Martin's Station before all of the wagons arrived. He decided to take them no farther. It was a wise move, for it was to be twenty years before the road would be improved enough for wagons to travel to Kentucky. Sheds were built, and the wagons and those supplies they were unable to load on the horses were left inside the fort.

By this time other groups heading for Kentucky had stopped here, and Henderson had welcomed them. All left Martin's together on April the fifth. Trouble began almost at once—so Henderson recorded in the journal he kept. Luttrell went out hunting and did not return. Two of the group went out to search for him. Then some of the horses bolted, bursting the wanties or ropes with which the pack saddles were tied and scattering supplies all over the ground.

One of the groups that had joined Henderson was having its troubles, too. The leader was a Welshman named William Calk, and he and his companions had suffered many difficulties in reaching Martin's Station. Calk kept a journal of their journey, too, and to add to the hardships of travel, he had great trouble with his punctuation and spelling.

". . . Come to a turabel mountain that tired us almost to death to git over it . . ." One of the "hors" had smashed three powder gourds, torn open a wallet of corn, and made "a turrabel flustration amongst the Reast of the Horses . . . (a) mair run against a sapling & noct it down we cacht them all agin & went on . . ." Then a "saddel turned & the load all fell" in the water as they crossed a creek. Everyone seemed to have troubles traveling through the wilderness.

Two days after their departure it was snowing, but they did not halt. They went slowly on toward Cumberland Gap. Luttrell had been found, but he was ahead of them, still hunting. He sent back a letter saying he had found a traveler in the woods who told him that five persons had been killed by Indians on the "raod to the Cantuckee." At once Nathaniel Hart and those with him turned back, saying they had better stay in Powell Valley and raise corn for those passing through.

Henderson had already recorded that Hart made "a poor Hand of Traveling," and in spite of the trouble he had caused, the colonel must have wished that Hart had remained with the group. This was no time to desert the Transylvania colony.

The worst news was to arrive later that day in a letter from Daniel Boone. He had found two settlers in the woods "killed and sculped." Then Indians had attacked his road-cutters, killing two and badly wounding another.

He begged Henderson to hurry, as the men were very uneasy and needed cheering up. Boone added that now was "the time to flusterate" the red men, for if "we give way to them now, it will ever be the case."

The colonel pondered. Should he turn back? Did he have enough men with him to add to Boone's few and so "flusterate" the savages? He didn't know. He was a town man and not handy with a rifle at all. So were many others in his party. At this point Henderson might have remembered Dragging Canoe's prophecy that the settling of Kentucky would be bloody. Was it worth more bloodshed to establish his colony?

4

"A Dark Cloud"

Richard Henderson decided he would go on to Kentucky. He was determined not to give up his colony. He had already risked his fortune in this enterprise. He would risk his life as well. Daniel Boone needed help, and Henderson was going to bring it.

Could he persuade the men to follow him? Most of them were already worried over the thought that the red men might be waiting in ambush along the road ahead. Coming from east of the Blue Ridge, they were not accustomed to fighting Indians. Like Nathaniel Hart, they might turn and bolt at the first sign of danger. Henderson would have to call them together, to reassure them and ask them to trust him and to keep on with the journey.

It was an ideal spot for a speech. Overhead towered the Cumberland Mountains, their sides still patched with the morning's snow. Around the camp the tulip poplars had put out their soft pale green leaves. The hickory buds were fat, the maples in seed, and the shadblow and red-bud colored the woods with white and purplish sprays.

The colonel must have enjoyed speaking, much as the Indians had at his treaty. He certainly had made many a speech as a lawyer and listened to countless others as a judge. His letters were written in what seems now a stilted and overelegant style, yet at that time it was the accepted form, and his speeches must have been full of the same bombastic phrases. Whatever he said, it was probably very stirring, for afterward all the men agreed to rush as fast as possible to Boone.

They packed and passed on down the little valley and along the base of Pinnacle Mountain "with good courage." Then they began the sharp climb to the gap. In 1750, while exploring for land, Dr. Thomas Walker had come on the Warrior's Path. He had followed it and discovered this gap through the mountain range. Here, too, he had found a cave, and so it was natural for him to name this passageway Cave Gap. Proceeding through it, he came to a river, which he promptly named in honor of the Duke of Cumberland. In time the name Cumberland was also attached to the gap and to the mountain range.

Henderson knew it as Cumberland Gap. His party passed through and on the western slope beyond descended along a ravine. There they met forty men fleeing from Kentucky "on acct. of the Late Murder by the Indians." The colonel realized this would never do. He talked to the newcomers, trying desperately to persuade them to return to Kentuck with his own group. Only one agreed to do so. The rest hurried off eastward, taking several of the Virginians from Henderson's party with them.

Seeing that his followers' small supply of courage was waning, Henderson urged the men forward along the trail with greater speed. He himself was "on thorns to fly to Boone's assistance," yet the more he hurried the group, the more bad fortune slowed them down. It rained steadily, and the path was almost too slippery to use. The creeks were high, and crossing them was a hazardous task. The cattle had trouble keeping up with the company, and often the men were forced to wait for them. Every now and then they killed a beef or two for what Calk called "alittel snack."

Nathaniel Hart returned, having decided he would take his chances with his business associates after all.

They met others leaving Kentucky, but one day they overtook a group under William Whitley traveling westward. And there were women and children with them. Henderson must have been cheered by this. A pioneer who took his family and his possessions with him into the wilderness would not usually fly at the first sign of danger. When he had no home to return to, he had greater reason to stay and defend his family and land.

Holding a baby in her lap, Mrs. Whitley rode a horse while the oldest child was tied behind her. They were having a difficult time with the animal on the rough road, and it stumbled and fell often, sending her and "her children all in a pile tied together for When One went all must go in that situation."

After Henderson passed this group, several of his men fired at a bear crossing the trail ahead of them. The colonel knew the women in Whitley's party would think the Indians had attacked and would be greatly alarmed. He sent a man back to explain the shots and to give some of the bear's meat to the Whitleys. It was a kindly and thoughtful action on the part of Henderson, burdened as he was with his own misfortunes and trying to keep his men going bravely forward.

It was "alowry morning" and raining when they reached the Cumberland River. The stream was swollen and swift. It would take the party some time to cross with the packs on rafts and to swim the animals over separately. Henderson was more fearful than ever that Boone would give up, thinking no one was coming to his assistance. After all, the hunter had left with his axmen before the treaty had been brought to a successful close. Boone had no way of knowing that the land had been purchased or that Henderson was following the trail he had blazed. A messenger would have to be sent to him at once. It would be a dangerous ride. Who from Henderson's men would go?

The colonel asked for volunteers, but the men answered they had "sufficient employ with the pack-horses." He could see that they would not have gone even if they had been totally idle. He begged and pleaded with them in vain.

Colonel Henderson stood in the rain at the edge of the Cumberland River and stared across its muddy, roiling surface. Over there lay the empire he had bought from the Cherokees along with its curse—there *was* "a dark cloud over that country."

5

Cold Water, Lean Meat, and No Bread

Once more Henderson asked for someone to take a letter to Boone. This time he offered twenty thousand acres of land to the person willing to go. Still no one stepped forward. The colonel implored them with tears in his eyes, saying he and his company were ruined.

Then William Cocke volunteered to go if someone would ride with him, and they would split the land between them. No one cared for this proposition either. Henderson was very worried, for the situation was exceedingly distressing. He begged Cocke to go on alone, and the young man finally agreed to do so.

The following day was again "alowry morning and very like for Rain," Calk noted in his journal. Still, it wasn't so bad that he couldn't go hunting while the rafts were being built and Cocke was getting ready to leave.

Perhaps it was the gloomy morning, perhaps it was that William Cocke had been thinking of his ride through the wild country with Indians all around, for his undertaking appeared a little more dangerous now that it was time to depart. Henderson gave him no time to back out, however. He outfitted Cocke with "a good Queen Ann's musket, plenty of ammunition, a tomahawk, a large cuttoe knife, a Dutch blanket, and no small quantity of jerked beef" and sent him off on a "tolerably good horse" for the hundred-and-thirty-mile ride.

Henderson's party crossed the Cumberland River early the next morning. As usual, the horses gave the most trouble. When finally the cattle were across and the pack-saddles reloaded, they moved off downstream through "Some turrabel cainbrakes." Calk was not so tired from fighting his way through ten miles of these brakes that he couldn't notice that night at camp that one of the men with him "Bakes Bread with out Washing his hands." Nevertheless, he probably ate his share, for bread was a rare treat for this traveling group.

The party struggled on. They crossed each small stream on a felled sapling called a "raccoon bridge," toting their packs over on this tree-bridge and making their animals swim across. At nights they took turns at sentry duty. Henderson found that tired men made poor sentries, and as frightened as they were in the daytime, they usually slept during their turn at guarding at night, each one feeling sure the Indians would not attack during his particular watch.

However, it was neither the wet weather nor the rough road that caused the greatest trouble. It was the fleeing men they met. Each had a terrible tale to tell about the brutalities of the Indians and how huge numbers of them were roaming the Kentucky country. Panic ran like wildfire through Henderson's camp. Many of his men left, saying they had to go home and convince their friends that they were still alive and unharmed. The colonel tried his best to keep them, but they were much too frightened.

Those who went on, Henderson believed, owed their bravery to a fear of shame. He didn't care why they stayed with him, just as long as they followed him across the many creeks and down the narrow ravines as fast as he could lead them. And in the midst of all the trouble with desertions, the colonel recorded in his journal, "lost an ax this morn at Camp." At such a time this seems much too insignificant a thing to write down till one realizes what an expensive and useful tool an ax was to the pioneer. It might cost as much as he could earn for a week's work. That Henderson put it down with the other bits of misfortune showed how much it was valued.

No matter what happened to them, the colonel kept them going. The weather might be "rany" and the group make only five miles during a day's travel. Still, every mile behind them was a help. And some days they did manage to cover as much as twenty-two miles. Other times they were slowed by frequent crossings of the streams. Calk in disgust said that he knew they had gone back and forth through one single creek "about 50 times Some with very bad foards."

Between the frequent rains and the many fordings, the men stayed wet, those who rode as well as those who led the overloaded pack horses. All were covered with mud from the "very mire Road." And they were hungry. The cattle had long since been killed and eaten. The corn that was left had to be saved to make a crop when they reached Boone's Fort—if they ever got there. Most were discouraged and fearful of ever getting there. The chance to see a wonderful new country and to make a settlement was no longer the "dazzling object" it had been at the beginning of the journey.

Only Henderson remained firm in his belief that everything would be all right. He was philosophical about their misfortunes, saying, "Few enterprises of great consequence continue at all times to wear a favorable aspect." And the Transylvania colony was of the greatest importance to the country and to each individual, he reminded them. They were all partners in a great event and should be cheerful and brave.

Thus he led them on, off the Wilderness Road and northward toward the Kentucky River. This was the part of the trail that was entirely new, laid out by Boone himself. The main Wilderness Road went on westward across Kentucky, following the ancient Indian path toward the falls of the Ohio River. One day the men were surprised in camp by a wolf and another day were overjoyed at meeting four of Boone's helpers sent to them with "excellent beef in plenty." There was news, too. William Cocke had ridden safely through the wilderness. Boone had held his ground and had not lost any of the valuable supplies to the savages. And there had been no more raids by the northern Indians.

The men felt greatly encouraged. They might, after all, get a sight of the meadows of sweet clover where there were so many buffaloes that they appeared as one vast herd. The colonel relaxed too and began to look about him at the country. He noted an ideal place for a mill and the good tracts of land along the stream bottoms or the "weak land" timbered with oak. They came to the mouth of Otter Creek and turned and followed the Kentucky River downstream to the spot Daniel Boone had chosen for the capital of the Transylvania colony. They arrived about noon and were welcomed by "a running fire of about 25 guns."

Richard Henderson had made it safely with his men after a month of travel "in a barren desert country" over a road that was "either hilly, stony, slippery, miry or bushy." It was April the twentieth, warm and sunny, and he was forty years old that day. His colony was going to succeed. He was here to take charge and see that it did. Then he sat down to a dinner of "cold water and lean buffalo meat, without bread." And never, never in his life had a meal tasted so good to him as that one eaten there on his own domain.

6

A Dream within a Dream

By the following day Richard Henderson was beginning to suspect that all was not as booming at Boone's Fort as had appeared on his arrival. Boone might be a keen hunter, an excellent tracker of Indians, and a master road blazer, but he was certainly no judge of a good and proper site for a town.

In the first place the Kentucky River valley here was much too narrow for a growing town. Too, the ground was low and would undoubtedly be flooded with each freshet. The colonel decided to pick a spot about three hundred yards away and on higher ground. There he would build a strong fort and call it Boonesborough. The defensive work Boone had begun wasn't much. The stockade was not completed, and the cabins had been hastily thrown up and looked as if they might fall in the first hard wind. Boone couldn't handle the men. Three days' work from them and the fort would be finished, yet he had been unable to make any of them do the work. Cocke reported it was in this bad shape when he had arrived. Henderson could see that if the Indians attacked, they would all be doomed, for the fort was useless as it stood now.

He set about trying to persuade the men to get to work on it, but he was no more successful than Boone. They had no idea of subordination. Each tended to his own private business first. William Calk went fishing and caught three catfish, then he set about getting his house "kivered with bark." Most of the men went off to look for good land, hunting along the way if they chanced upon the tracks of a stray buffalo or an elk. The colonel could not get too much cooperation from his business associates either. Hart was not the least bit interested in helping. Luttrell moved off to his own land, though he did leave a couple of men to help Henderson with the work.

The colonel was disappointed that the others were not inspired as he was to try to maintain the interest and security of each and every inhabitant. He worked hard and managed to get his corn planted, the seed sown in his garden, and a magazine built to protect the powder. He also marked off town lots and had the men draw for them. The number of divergent, daily tasks he performed was enormous—letters to his partners and to many others, keeping the company's account books, and trying desperately to find enough food from his garden to stay alive. Since the settlers had taken over the salt springs in the little valley, the game had stopped coming there. Now a man had to go as much as twenty-five miles away from the fort to hunt. Henderson was no hunter. He had to depend on whatever was given him or what he could trade for, or he had to do without. Once he noted: "Almost starved. Drank a little coffee & trust to luck for dinner."

And yet these problems were not the ones that worried the colonel the most. Land titles! That was what bothered him night and day. Those who had already settled in Kentucky before Henderson's arrival claimed the land by right of being there first. Others said Kentucky belonged to Virginia and that colony had warned all to beware of Henderson and his company. Every day newcomers drifted through the country, marking out land for themselves by blazing trees with a tomahawk or hoping to hold a tract by planting a crop of corn on it. Then they took off again or sold their "Tomahawk rights" or became dissatisfied with what they first found and searched out better land and took that. Land claims were beginning to overlap each other like shingles on a roof, and these "shingled" claims were going to confuse and involve every settler in endless legal arguments unless something was devised to stop the practice at once.

And though Richard Henderson understood all too well what was taking place, he did not know what to do. He had expected his rule to be supreme. This was his domain. He had bought it. Yet he had no way of making these squatters recognize his authority. Many were "Lawless people from habit and Education," and they would laugh in his face if he told them to leave *his* property.

He had to take some kind of action, nevertheless, or his whole colonization scheme would fail. What could he possibly suggest to these bold and spirited frontier settlers that would gain their approval of and their allegiance to Transylvania? He thought much about this and at last decided that the simplest plan was to have a convention of members of the four separated and distinct settlements.

Selected by free choice, these delegates from Harrods-burg, Boiling Springs, St. Asaph, and Boonesborough could meet and make their own laws. They could then bind themselves to obey and execute these same laws, and with the help of the officials of the Transylvania Company, a government could begin.

This met with approval. The representatives of the four settlements were chosen, and they met at Boonesborough under "a divine elm" that stood in the middle of a meadow of clover. It was a huge tree, four feet through at the trunk, with the first limbs beginning higher up the bole than a man could reach. The branches extended in a good fifty-foot radius. In the shadow of this elm the Kentucky settlers drew up their laws. Henderson read a speech full of flowery phrases and sentimental rhetoric. Afterwards, he took possession of the land in an ancient and feudal ceremony called "Livery and Seizin."

The attorney employed by the Cherokees at Sycamore Shoals was there. He cut from the ground a large piece of sod, and he handed this to Henderson. While they both held the turf in their hands, the attorney declared his de-livery of seizin, or possession of the land, to Henderson in accordance with the terms of the title deed. Then the colonel read the terms of the deed aloud to the seated delegates. Though this was an obsolete English ceremony and seldom performed in American legal practice, it was a shrewd move for Henderson to make. It gave him the chance to have his deed recorded officially, along with all that took place at the convention, and perhaps to pro-tect his purchase against land grabbers.

It also gave him the means to hold the center of the stage for a moment. And it was a very proud moment for Richard Henderson. Reverently he took the turf from the attorney and held it up for all to see, as though in that one piece of Kentucky sod were all the years of hard work and talk and money he had given to developing a settlement on the Western Waters. His triumph had arrived.

Henderson's happiness soon began to fade. The men at Harrodsburg decided their future prospects would be much better as Virginia citizens than as Transylvanians. They spread rumors against the Henderson company and created so much unrest among Kentucky settlers that the colony's planned second gathering of delegates was called off. Then Harrodsburg called its own assembly and elected two men to take a signed petition to Virginia, asking that state to assume its rightful duty under its original charter and govern Kentucky.

By the end of 1776, Virginia agreed to assume this responsibility and created Kentucky County, its westernmost jurisdiction. This was bitter for Richard Henderson, yet it was not the death blow to his colony. He still had a claim to the soil of Transylvania, and for two more years he fought to make that claim legal. At that time Virginia passed a resolution that made private purchase of Indian land unlawful. The Transylvania colony was now dead and gone forever.

However, its capital survived for a while. The Boonesborough fort was part of Kentucky's defenses during the Revolution against the northern Indians and their British allies, and it did not fall once. After the war the settlement began to grow. By the time Kentucky was admitted to the Union, Boonesborough was one of the largest cities in the state. But soon thereafter a decline set in, and each year found fewer and fewer people living there. At last the town disappeared altogether. Its location, so proudly chosen by Boone, so happily bought by Henderson, ended as a lonely part of a river farm.

Still Colonel Henderson was never one to give up. He had secured some fine land along the Cumberland River in his huge purchase. It was south of Virginia's boundary. He pressed settlers into going there and living around the French Salt Lick. It was not long before North Carolina took those lands from him, but the settlement thrived and became Nashville, Tennessee, the capital of that state. Some worthless hilly lands were finally given to the Transylvania Company by North Carolina, and Virginia also ceded the company a tract of not too good land. Both these tracts were given in recognition of the company's efforts in promoting colonization in the Dark and Bloody Land. But it mattered not to Richard Henderson. He had died before then, in 1785, disappointed that he had little to show for the last twelve years of his life, the time that he had devoted to the Transylvania colony. His dream of an empire had failed in a land that had for such a long period been a fabulous and dreamlike place itself.

~ *Part Six* ~

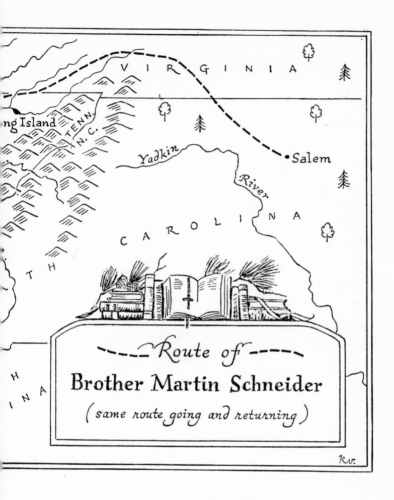

VIRGINIA

TENN. N.C.

ng Island

Yadkin

River

• Salem

CAROLINA

T H

I N A

-- - - Route of - - - --

Brother Martin Schneider

(same route going and returning)

kv.

Martin Schneider, Moravian brother, and his trials and efforts when attempting to get a Cherokee agreement to a mission in 1783.

1

"The Heart Is Fixed and Trusteth in God"

The man on the horse was lost. The trail he had been following all afternoon to the Cherokee towns had vanished at last under a white blanket. He came to a halt, glancing back. The snow was falling so fast that it had almost filled the marks of the horse's last few steps. Night would soon be here. There was no place where he could stay and be protected from the damp and bitter cold. What was he to do?

He could no more return than he could go forward. To move at all through the woods, half-blinded by the snow, was to risk riding over a cliff or falling in a stream. Still, he couldn't sit here astride his beast all night long.

The horse snorted and tossed its head to shake away the wet, clinging snow. It stamped and shifted about uneasily. The man leaned forward and patted the animal soothingly while he pondered his situation.

More than anything, he yearned for his mission to the Indians to succeed. He hoped to get the Cherokees to agree that the Moravian brethren could come among them and spread the Glory of the Lord "on this dark country."

He had volunteered for this journey because he sincerely "believed that our Saviour would not have ap-

pointed this journey, if it had not been His hour for it."
Yet everything had gone wrong from the very first.

A government official had intended to accompany him
on the trail, but at the last minute sickness had prevented
it. The Indian agent could not be found at his quarters
on the Holston River. The missionary had gone on alone.
He had not wanted to return back across the Blue Ridge
Mountains to his home in Salem, North Carolina, and report failure.

Now he was lost. He was not a woodsman and therefore knew little of wilderness ways. All of his twenty-seven
years had been spent in Moravian settlements among
the church members.

He had learned how to make shoes, good sturdy, long-
lasting shoes. He knew how to farm. He could plow as
well as any man or take his turn at milking when the time
came. He could play church music on the trombone, too.
But none of those skills could help him now. He sat there
bewildered and undecided about what he should do.

Back in Salem, lights would at this moment be shining
cheerfully through the house windows. Here and there
would be the muffled sounds of violins or flutes or horns
as the various brothers practiced their music. From the
kitchen would come the sounds of the sisters preparing
supper. And as a door opened, the smell of hot wheat
bread or pork dumplings or cooking turnips might escape
to mingle with the cold night air.

Children would be packing snowballs, bombarding each
other across the unused town lots and among the houses

on their way home from choir practice or from school. There might be a love feast at the minister's house for a Moravian brother visiting from Pennsylvania. And through the twilight would come the squeaking of the mill wheel as the last turn of corn was run or the last of the flint rocks were ground into powder for use as a glaze in the pottery shed.

The man gave a start as the horse pulled sharply at the reins and whickered with irritation. He tightened up on the lines. The snow was falling much harder now. He could see but a few feet beyond the animal's head. It would be foolhardy to ride on, floundering through the trees and bushes. Yet he could not make a shelter for himself here.

Perhaps he was going to die at this place. Perhaps the Lord was angry with him for his impatience and arrogance in making the journey by himself. Maybe he should have accepted the Lord's will and meekly turned back to Salem when it became clear that no one would guide him to the Cherokees. Perhaps he had committed the sin of pride in going on.

And then perhaps not. Perhaps the Lord had meant to test him by setting him all these obstacles.

He bowed his head and began to pray aloud in German. He told of his troubles and of the dangers of the coming night. He asked for help, laying his "concern on the faithful heart of our dr. Savr. represented to Him that it was his Affair, & prayed him to be himself my dr. Fellow Traveller."

When he had finished, he pulled the collar of his great
coat up around his ears. Blinking away the snowflakes
caught in his eyelashes, he gently nudged the horse in
the ribs with his heels. It did not move.

He began to talk to the animal, trying to coax it into a
walk. It was not to be afraid. Everything would be all
right. The man assured the horse that when "the heart
is fixed and trusteth in God," there was no need to worry
or to fret.

At last the horse stepped forward, feeling its way carefully. The man took a deep breath and began to sing:

> "Who waits until the Saviour leads,
> Will see the joy intended;
> No anxious questions will he need
> With difficulties ended."

When he finished this hymn, he felt comforted. Singing it had brought a warmth to his chilled body. He began
another Moravian song, the liturgy "O Head So Full of
Bruises."

They had not gone far, however, pushing through the
bushes and under the low hanging limbs, when the horse
stumbled and fell to its knees. The man stayed astride it.
The animal struggled to its feet, but it refused to go on.
It stood there snorting and trembling.

There was only a little light left. He should be worried
about a shelter, he knew, yet he wasn't. He seemed to
feel the presence of the Lord there with him in the wilderness, and he was unafraid.

Suddenly from a long way off, he heard the wind roaring. The sound grew louder and louder. Then the air raced past horse and rider, swirling the snow this way and that, and died in the distance.

Through a rift in the falling snow the man saw something that made his heart leap. He climbed down from his horse and stiffly made his way there, leading the animal. He was right! It was a hollow tree! And it leaned so that there was a fine dry place at its base for him to spend the night. It had been used for this purpose before, for the inside was charred black.

He tied the horse to a little dogwood tree, and it began to eat the winter buds. From the saddlebag the man took flint, steel, a piece of tow cloth, and a handful of dry wood chips. He knew how to make a fire. It was the same in the wilderness as it was at Salem, although it was much easier in the town to go to your neighbor and borrow hot coals from his fire to begin your own.

He struck the metal with the flintstone until a spark landed on the tow cloth and began to smolder. He blew on it till it blazed and added the chips. With some limbs from a nearby fallen tree, he built up the fire in the opening till it was hot and bright inside the hollow tree.

Taking out his Bible, he read a few verses. Afterwards he thanked the Saviour for showing him this place in which he could spend the night. Then he made some coffee and ate the corn-meal journey cake he had brought with him. He gave a piece of the corn bread to the horse, for it was all he had for his mount.

After he had spread his blanket at the back of the tree, he got out his journal and pen and ink. Sitting cross-legged, he looked at the page and read aloud part of the heading: "Journey of Brother Martin Schneider from Salem to Long Island on the Holston and from there . . ." His first entry had been December 15, 1783.

If he returned safely to his home in Salem, this report would be given to the elders of the church. It might eventually end up in the library with the other Moravian diaries and records written long ago, some about journeys such as his, others being the daily records of the towns and churches.

He smiled happily. That would be a very satisfying and blessed thing to happen to him. It would unite him with the Moravian brothers of the past and with those who might read his report in the future, all working to serve Him who died on the Cross.

Dipping his quill in the inkhorn, he began to write that day's happenings on the paper: "The 29th in the morning my Horse was nowhere to be seen. I looked . . . "

2

"A Music-Loving People"

Thirty years before Martin Schneider began his journey across the Blue Ridge to the Cherokees, fifteen unmarried men left the Moravian town of Bethlehem in Pennsylvania. They were heading south to the colony of North Carolina, where close to ninety-nine thousand acres of land had been bought by the church for the beginning of another settlement.

Their farm wagon had been too wide for the double-rutted road they followed. So they had a smith cut three inches from one side. The wagon contained a tent, a grindstone, all their tools and possessions. Without it they were doomed. Yet, what a struggle it was to help the horses get the wagon up the steep hills and across the numerous streams and through the stretches of hindering mud.

In six weeks they reached their tract of land. Finding an abandoned cabin, they took possession of it. Though it was small and the roof was full of holes, there was enough room for all of them to lie down and sleep around the walls.

They made a fire on the hearth on their arrival and had "a little Lovefeast." This was a religious service, in which songs were sung and a simple meal of bread and tea or coffee was shared by the members. One of the songs they sang that November day in 1753 was composed on the spot:

> "We hold arrival Lovefeast here,
> In Carolina land,
> A Company of Brethren true,
> A little Pilgrim band,

Called by the Lord to be of those
Who through the whole world go,
To bear Him witness everywhere,
And naught but Jesus know."

While their voices rang out, the wolves howled around
the cabin. But the brethren sang on for their hearts were
full of thanksgiving to the Saviour.

Music was a vital part of their lives. They often were
awakened with music in the mornings or sang hymns
on arising. They sang while they worked and at the
table. On solemn occasions and at festivals a set of trom-
bones from Europe was used, and these "strengthened and
edified" the congregation. A visiting brother would tell
those in North Carolina what music was popular in Pennsylvania and would sing the new tunes to the congregation to the accompaniment of their only two violins so
that all could learn it.

The brethren had been in North Carolina only three
months before one of them made a trumpet out of a
hollow tree limb. It was promptly put to use to call them
to a Sabbath Lovefeast, and as their historian wrote in
the diary: "No trumpet in Bethlehem had a better tone."

But these "music-loving people" could work, too. Four
of the brothers of the original group returned to Pennsylvania. The eleven who stayed in North Carolina began
their labors at once. They had been hand-picked for the
new colony because of their qualifications. One was a
shoemaker, another a tailor. There was a doctor, as well
as "a man whom all animals love." Each, however, had a

number of skills, and each was willing to do anything required to make this Moravian settlement succeed.

One of the first tasks the doctor had to perform was an operation. He removed a bone splinter embedded in a backwoodsman's head one morning. By that same afternoon he was digging a wolf pit. The tailor was paid to make a pair of breeches for a traveler passing through. But when not sewing, he worked all day splitting rails or chasing through the briars after a straying horse or washing the dirty pots.

From the one wagon came axes, a plow, needle, thread, a scalpel, grubbing hoes, hymn books, and Bibles. With these and with hard work the eleven brothers had in a few years a thriving community. Where once had stood scrub oak and tall pine trees, there was now a bakery, a mill, a tavern, a potter's shop, and many other buildings for various crafts.

With the colony firmly established, the married members of the church came with their families. Then other settlements were begun. When the land was bought, plans had been made for a town in the center of the large tract. This town became Salem, the home of Martin Schneider.

One of the aims of the Moravians in settling in the wilds of North Carolina had been to be near the southern Indians so that they could preach the Gospel to them. They had tried many times to begin this work, but they had been "frustrated by the Wars and Bickerings between them and the neighboring white Settlers."

Through their settlements the Moravians had felt that

the Saviour meant to bless the Cherokees. Now in 1783 they were ready to establish a mission among these Indians. First though, they needed the red men's permission, and Brother Martin Schneider had been sent to get it.

3

Old Corn Tassel

Brother Schneider survived the December night in the hollow tree. He kept warm and dry, but he was "dyed pretty black" from the smoke and from rubbing against the charcoal interior of the leaning tree. The following day he was able to find his way through the snow back to the nearest cabin. There he hired a guide.

By January the third he crossed the Little Tennessee River to the Cherokee town "called Sitiko." The name has been spelled various ways, Citico, Settico, and so on. Though the Indian agent lived here, it must have been quite a small town at this time.

Chota, the capital and home of the head chief, Old Corn Tassel, was mentioned by Schneider as being one of the largest towns on the river, and it had only thirty houses plus the additional hothouses. But it, too, was just a remnant of its former size.

The Cherokees were no longer the great nation they

had been at the beginning of the eighteenth century, when the Old Rabbit traded with them. Then there were at least sixty towns with a fighting force estimated at from four to six thousand warriors. Now there were no fighting men in the towns along the Little Tennessee. The Cherokees had sided with the British in the Revolution. When the Americans destroyed a great number of their villages in the Valley and Middle settlements, the older chiefs of the Overhill Towns along the Little Tennessee begged to be peaceful neutrals for the remainder of the war. Dragging Canoe and his young braves were furious. They wanted to keep fighting with the British. So in 1777, they left the nation and established towns of their own along Chickamauga Creek. Supplied by the British, the Canoe sent out his war parties from there to harass the American settlers. His splinter war group was called Chickamaugas, to distinguish it from the peaceful Cherokees.

A flotilla of frontiersmen floated down the Tennessee River and destroyed the Chickamauga towns. Dragging Canoe was not discouraged. He took his people southward into the wilderness, where the mountains and the rapids of the Tennessee gave him much better protection. He and his Chickamaugas lived in what was known as The Five Lower Towns and continued their warfare against the Americans. At Brother Schneider's visit what was left of the peaceful faction of the Cherokee nation was in decline. They were changing to the white man's way of living. Since so much of their hunting land was gone, they were turning to farming and to livestock raising. They wore the white man's clothes most of the time, not just for "dressed up" occasions. They no longer built their houses the Indian way. Now they had notched log cabins, "blocked up of narrow logs . . . and the Chimney fixed on the outside."

At Sitiko, Brother Schneider found Joseph Martin, the Indian agent, and he explained his mission. A meeting of the chiefs was arranged for two days later.

While he waited, the Moravian brother visited the nearby towns. He was received with friendliness everywhere. He ate bread made of pounded corn, beans, and roasted pumpkins. At one house there was a group of Indians sitting around a kettle of "dried and boiled peaches." He was offered some and had to dig into the pot with his fingers just as the Indians were doing. It must have been hard for Brother Schneider, used to the spotless Moravian kitchens. He observed that their pots and dishes were never washed "otherwise than by the licking of the Dogs."

He wanted to learn the Cherokee language, but he made little progress. Though the Cherokees understood English, they would not speak it. And Schneider's German accent must have added to the difficulties. He did find out that "they have no Words for cursing & swearing, & therefore make Use of the English."

When the day for the meeting came, it was held in the house of the interpreter, James McCormick, an old man who had been living with the Cherokees for some time. In former days the meeting would have taken place in the council house with all the proper ceremonies around the sacred fire.

Here it was very informal, with the few chiefs sitting cross-legged on the floor facing the white men. Colonel Martin began by telling the Indians about the Moravian Church. He knew one of the merchants in Salem and was familiar with their religious beliefs. He told that the Moravians did not believe in fighting and would never "meddle with War." He explained their trust in God and their love for the Saviour and their belief that religion was a necessary part of everyday life.

The Indian agent then told them that Brother Schneider was there to ask permission for his brethren to come and live among the Cherokees. They would not trade or take away the Indians' land, as most white men did, but would teach them about God, their Creator.

Brother Schneider watched the Indians' faces, but he could not tell how they were taking all this. The head chief, sitting with the others, seemed not to be listening. Brother Schneider prayed silently that they would vote for the mission. The Cherokees needed help. At the houses where he had stayed coming here, he could tell that the white settlers "scarce look upon them as human creatures."

The interpreter spoke for the mission, too, telling the Cherokees how much they could be helped by the Moravians. He talked with emotion, preaching a little about how the brothers were concerned about the Indians'

souls and their salvation, about how the brothers wanted
the Indians happy now and hereafter.

The chiefs shifted restlessly on the floor. McCormick's
Indian wife came in and built up the fire. Brother
Schneider leaned forward anxiously. It was Old Tassel's
time to speak.

The head chief arose slowly. He was heavy-set with "a
smooth and somewhat fat and inflated face." He was
never known to lie and therefore was much respected by
the white officials. He spoke well, and Brother Schneider
wished he understood Cherokee so there would be none
of the stopping for interpretation.

Old Tassel said for himself he would be glad to have
the brothers come and "tell them of Utajah (God) that
great Man who dwells above." But he had to wait till all
the chiefs and braves were back from their winter hunts.
When they returned, he would call "a great meeting to
Hear their Mind" and would let the good brother know
what they decided.

The meeting was over. Brother Schneider felt disappointed. But Colonel Martin said he had not expected so
favorable an answer.

There was nothing more to be done. Brother Schneider
wanted to start back for Salem at once. But the weather
was very cold, and the rain of yesterday had turned into
snow today. The river was high and much too dangerous
to try to ford, he was told.

He waited a few days. He visited the Indian families.
He prayed. He read the Daily Word. This was a verse

of the Old Testament listed for reading on each day of the year. That particular day it was: "When thou passest through the Waters I will be with thee."

When Brother Schneider read that, he was determined to leave the next day, even if the water had not receded. Colonel Martin was not able to go with him, as planned.

"I will set out tomorrow alone," the brother said. "My waiting here is to no further purpose."

4

A Man of Ice and Snow

The following morning Brother Schneider was up early to pray. In the stillness he had his "Hour of Intercession." One of his prayers was for the Indians. He "recommended once more with particular Concern the Situation of the poor Cherokees to the faithful Heart of our Savr."

His prayers over, he bid Colonel Martin farewell and left. The river here was too deep to ford. He crossed it in a canoe, and his horse swam over behind the boat. Then he rode north across the snowy landscape. By the afternoon of the second day he had reached the French Broad River. He could not find the fording place in the drifted snow. There was nothing for Brother Schneider to do but prepare for the coming night.

He had just kindled a fire when some passing settlers

offered to show him the fording place. He left with them quickly, forgetting to take his tow and chips. There was still some daylight left. The Moravian was determined to cross the river, for he wanted to reach Salem as quickly as possible.

He urged his horse down the bank. It broke through the ice at the edge and then balked at going out into the swift current. But at last it began to move out into the stream toward a large island. The water became deeper and deeper, but Brother Schneider let the animal pick its way cautiously across. He held up his feet and kept dry, for the horse was able to wade the whole way.

However, it had taken him longer to reach the island than he had expected. Darkness was almost upon him. Brother Schneider stared across the yellow swirling water. Should he attempt the rest of the crossing now? No, it was much too dangerous in the poor light. He would spend the night on the island.

He led his horse to the end of the island, disturbing a flock of geese and swans sleeping there. The big geese flew up and circled over him, honking loudly. The swans were not so frightened of the two intruders as the other birds and only edged slowly away with hoarse cries of "Beep, beep!"

Without his tow and dry chips Brother Schneider had a difficult time making a fire, and it was midnight before he succeeded. As he sat beside the blaze drinking his coffee, there was a sudden hissing and spluttering, and clouds of steam arose. Brother Schneider jumped to his feet. The river was rising. The water had reached one side of his fire.

He took what was left of the burning brands and moved farther back on the island. He didn't know whether he would be safe here or not. The water was already over the end of the island and lapping steadily closer and closer to him. He slept little that night.

By morning the river had almost reached his fire a second time. He had to get off the island. He studied the roaring, rushing water. It was much swifter today. The noise was terrifying. Huge trees floated past and cakes of swirling ice.

Brother Schneider was frightened. Never in his life had he encountered anything as dangerous as this. There was only one thing to do—he began to pray. He had a "quite peculiar conversation" with the Saviour. He said he knew he deserved the Saviour's displeasure in many ways. "But I begged it as a Favour to help me thro' this Water."

Then he took off some of his clothes in case he had to swim, strapped them to the saddlebag, and mounted his horse. The animal was more reluctant than ever, but after much urging, it eased into the water, straining to keep its feet as the full force of the current hit it.

Step by uncertain step, they moved away from the island. It looked as if they might make the other bank without any trouble. Suddenly two great chunks of ice came bobbing toward them. Brother Schneider managed to push one away with his foot, but the other cake slammed into the horse's side. It lost its footing and was swept downstream into deep water.

The horse floundered about, snorting in terror but struggling valiantly to swim. Brother Schneider stayed astride it, but as the animal sank lower and lower, it was all he could do to keep his head above the surface.

They sped along, now close to the bank, where the cliffs were "straight as a wall," now hurled violently out into midstream. And there ahead of them was a huge rock, jagged and sharp. They hurtled toward it at a great speed. Brother Schneider tried to guide the horse to one side of it. The animal was tired. It could hardly keep its head out of the water.

The brother held onto the horse's mane and, floating out behind the animal, began to kick his feet, trying to steer them to one side. They missed the rock and went shooting along under the bluffs. Then the horse found its footing and they were across the river and safe from drowning.

Brother Schneider searched for a way up the cliffs. He found a "narrow pass" for himself, but he had to leave his horse standing in the water. He broke through the ice to the bank and climbed up the passageway. In his wet clothes he began to run. Over the hills and through the snow he jogged, and "all was to me like a dream." But he was so happy to be alive that he gave thanks as he ran to "our Savr. for his Wonderful help."

After three miles he reached a cabin and knocked on the door. A woman opened the door and screamed at what she saw, for on her threshold stood a man of ice and snow—poor shivering Brother Schneider, coatless and frozen into his wet clothes.

5

"The Dutch Fort, Where There Are Good People and Much Bread"

Brother Schneider was taken care of, his horse was rescued, and by the following day both were traveling again. Soon he crossed the Blue Ridge, and by January 24 he had reached his "beloved congregation Salem, my journey ended, and full of praise and thanks to my Saviour for the protection and mercy which He had vouchsafed me on my way."

It had been quite a journey for a town man unaccustomed to wilderness ways. And it must have made a deep impression on Martin Schneider. Eighteen years later on the anniversary of the day he had returned, he remembered to give thanks to the Lord for "returning from the Cherokees."

Not long after he was safely home, his journal was read to all the Moravian congregations in North Carolina. All rejoiced, for it seemed that at last their strong desire to proclaim the Gospel to the Indians was to be realized. Then Schneider's diary was sent to Europe to the Moravians there. The Moravians had churches and settlements all over the world, and they always sent each other important reports or travel journals.

At first Brother Schneider was hopeful that word would soon come from Old Corn Tassel. But he heard nothing as the months went by. Colonel Martin passed through Salem one day and said the Cherokees spoke often of Brother Schneider, but there was not a thing said about a mission.

Brother Schneider was disappointed. But at least he could console himself with the fact that he had not met the fate of an early Presbyterian visitor among the Indians. This minister "preached scripture till both his audience and he were heartily tired." Then he was told by the Cherokees "that they knew very well, that, if they were good, they should go up; if bad, down; that he could tell no more; that he had long plagued them with what they no ways understood, and that they desired him to depart the country."

However, it was not until 1803 that a mission was finally established for the Cherokees and one soon thereafter for the Creeks. During all these years the Moravians always treated the Indians passing through their settlements with respect. They would invite the visiting red men to their singing services. Or they would play the organ for them. And always the Moravians fed them.

For the Indians, as for the backwoods settlers, corn bread was the staple food. But once the braves had eaten wheat or rye bread baked by the Moravians, they developed a fondness for it. From the earliest times the Moravian settlement in North Carolina had been described by the Cherokees as "the Dutch fort, where there are good people and much bread." *Deutsch* means German, but it had been corrupted into Dutch by the English-speaking neighbors of the Moravians. The Indians had picked up the word from these white settlers.

Brother Schneider had been close to a successful beginning when he attempted to learn the language of the Cherokees. The Moravians in Pennsylvania had done missionary work among the northern Indians for years, and that was the method they used.

"First to learn the language. . . . The Indians are always agreeable to a desire to learn their language and like to see it written down." But never ask "permission of the Chiefs to preach the Gospel. If one begins with the Chiefs, the answer may be known in advance: 'We will think about it, and, if we agree, we will let you know.' That will never happen."

Old Corn Tassel had used just such a ruse.

Brother Schneider, though he had "felt unworthiness," had undertaken his journey to the Cherokees in spite of dangers and hardships because he genuinely desired to help the Indians. The Moravians were all honest, upright, and kindhearted people. Though they were small in numbers in the Old Southwest, they were large in purpose, and wherever they went, they succeeded in bringing contentment and light with them.

A Word After

So here are some of the people who ventured into the American wilderness, leaving behind the safer settlements along the seaboard. They were many different kinds of people, and they went for all sorts of reasons. I have tried to show you the main reason each of these made his perilous journey. However, with the exception of Mrs. Inglis, each of them had more than one reason. Selflessness was mixed with a little greed, business was confused with some pleasure, and I expect plain old curiosity played a good part in every man's decision to "go west."

America was and is a big country and a varied country. That's why it took so many different kinds of folks to explore it and settle it and to make it the great nation it is today. Those differences were important then and they are important now.

Each of us, in his own way, sets out to explore the wilderness of the future that lies ahead. We go different ways and we go for different reasons, but all those ways and reasons are needful and necessary if we are to plunge farther into space, delve deeper into the atom, and expand in human understanding. If we were all alike and all went the same way, vast regions of the future would never be explored or mapped or hunted over or settled.

Bibliography

Section 1

BACKGROUND MATERIAL

Brown, John P. *Old Frontiers*. Kingsport: Southern Publishers, 1938.

Crane, Verner W. *The Southern Frontier, 1670-1732*. Ann Arbor: University of Michigan Press, 1956.

Hale, John P. *Trans-Allegheny Pioneers*. Cincinnati: The Graphic Press, 1886.

Kincaid, Robert L. *The Wilderness Road*. Indianapolis: Bobbs-Merrill Co., 1947.

Lester, William Stewart. *The Transylvania Colony*. Spencer: Samuel R. Guard & Co., 1935.

Meriwether, Robert L. *The Expansion of South Carolina, 1729-1765*. Kingsport: Kingsport Press, 1940.

Mooney, James. *Myths of the Cherokee*. (Nineteenth Annual Report of the Bureau of American Ethnology.) Washington: Government Printing Office, 1900.

Myer, William E. *Indian Trails of the Southeast*. (Forty-second Annual Report of the Bureau of American Ethnology.) Washington: Government Printing Office, 1928.

Pusey, William Allen. *The Wilderness Road to Kentucky*. New York: George H. Doran Co., 1921.

Swanton, John R. *Early History of the Creek Indians and Their Neighbors.* (Bulletin 73 of the Bureau of American Ethnology.) Washington: Government Printing Office, 1922.

————. *The Indians of the Southeastern United States.* (Bulletin 137 of the Bureau of American Ethnology.) Washington: Government Printing Office, 1946.

Williams, Samuel Cole. *Dawn of Tennessee Valley and Tennessee History.* Johnson City: The Watauga Press, 1937.

————. *Early Travels in the Tennessee Country, 1540-1800.* Johnson City: The Watauga Press, 1928.

Section II

SOURCE MATERIAL FOR QUOTATIONS

Adair, James. *History of the American Indians.* London: E. & C. Dilly, 1775.

Allen, Joel A. *The American Bisons, Living and Extinct.* (*Memoirs of the Museum of Comparative Zoology,* Harvard College, Vol. IV, No. 10.) Cambridge: Cambridge University Press, 1876.

Carroll, Bartholomew Rivers (ed. and comp.). *Historical Collections of South Carolina.* New York: Harper & Brothers, 1836.

Chicken, George. *Journal of the March of the Carolinians into the Cherokee Mountains, 1715-1716.* (*Year Book of the City of Charleston,* Langdon Cheves, ed.) Charleston: 1894.

Christopher Gist's Journals. Notes by William M. Darlington. Cleveland: The Arthur H. Clark Co., 1893.

Crevecoeur, J. Hector St. John. *Letters from an American Farmer.* London: T. Davies, 1782.

Doddridge, Joseph. "Notes on the Settlement and Indian Wars of the Western Parts of Virginia and Pennsylvania," in *A History of the Valley of Virginia* by Samuel Kercheval. Woodstock: J. Gatewood, 1850.

Drake, Samuel G. *Biography and History of the Indians of North America.* Boston: Benjamin B. Mussey & Co., 1851.

Fries, Adelaide L. (ed.). *Records of the Moravians in North Carolina,* Vols. I-VII. Raleigh: State Dept. of Archives and History, 1922-1947.

Haywood, John. *The Natural and Aboriginal History of Tennessee.* Nashville: George Wilson, 1823.

Hulbert, Archer Butler. *Boone's Wilderness Road.* Cleveland: A. H. Clark Co., 1903.

Johnston, J. Stoddard. *First Exploration of Kentucky.* Louisville: John P. Morton & Co., 1898.

Logan, John H. *A History of the Upper Country of South Carolina.* Charleston: S. G. Courtenay & Co., 1859.

McDowell, W. L. (ed.) *Journals of the Commissioners of the Indian Trade, 1710-1718.* Columbia: South Carolina Archives Department, 1955.

O'Callaghan, E. B. (ed.). *The Documentary History of New York,* Vol. IV. Albany: Weed, Parsons & Co., 1851.

Palmer, William P. (ed.). *Calendar of Virginia State Papers,* Vol. I. Richmond: 1875.

Perkins, James Handasyd. *Annals of the West*. Cincinnati: J. R. Albach, 1850.

Ranck, George W. *Boonesborough*. Louisville: J. P. Morton & Co., 1901.

Smith, James. *An Account of the Remarkable Occurences in the Life and Travels of Col. James Smith*. Notes by William M. Darlington. Cincinnati: R. Clarke & Co., 1870.

Smyth, J. F. D. *A Tour in the United States of America*. London: G. Robinson, 1784.

South Carolina *Gazette*.

Thwaites, Reuben Gold (ed.). *Early Western Travels*, Vol. I. Cleveland: The Arthur H. Clark Co., 1904.

Timberlake, Henry. *The Memoirs of Lieut. Henry Timberlake*. London: J. Ridley, 1765.

Waddell, Jos. A. *Annals of Augusta County, Virginia*. Staunton: C. Russell Caldwell, 1902.